Releasing Jenna

D0943094

Releasing Jenna

One Woman's Struggle
Raising an Abused Child

Alice E. Bonner

Honey Ridge Press

Copyright © 2022 by Alice E. Bonner

All rights reserved. No part of this publication may be reproduced, stored in a retrieval system, or transmitted in any form or by any means, electronic, mechanical, photocopying, recording, or otherwise, without the prior written permission of the copyright holder, except brief quotations used in a review.

Cover photo © Shutterstock/alphaspirit.it

Author photo by Nicole Daggs

Design by Meadowlark Publishing Services

Published by Honey Ridge Press
honeyridgepress@gmail.com

Manufactured in the United States of America

ISBN 979-8-9856171-0-8

Published 2022

To social workers everywhere
who diligently advocate for children
in impossible situations.

Contents

Preface

Much has been publicized about the poor quality of our foster care system: foster parents are untrained and unsupported; there aren't enough of them; children are often taken in by unqualified people who need extra income. Studies of youth who have left foster care show they are more likely than those in the general population to be homeless, drop out of high school, be unemployed, lack higher education, become pregnant at an early age, suffer from post-traumatic stress disorder, and be imprisoned.

What about the reasons why the kids are removed from their homes in the first place? We know that many of the children suffer abuse, trauma, and neglect, but we don't hear much about the parents themselves. Instead of placing the blame of foster care failings on "the system," perhaps the responsibility should land at the source: those parents who are incapable of raising healthy kids and who continually have more. My husband, Ric, has often said, "There should be a class required before people can have children. They would have to show up on time and do the work. Only then would they be allowed." His opinion is tongue in cheek, but it's an interesting thought.

What follows is one family's attempt to save a little girl who was terribly abused in all ways: physically, emotionally, and verbally. Jenna's story is her own, as is ours. Some names have been changed to avoid confusion, but the book is based on reality.

1

Rescue

My life took a ten-year detour with a single phone call. Moments before, I sat at my cluttered desk, gazing at stacks of papers. I worked as the College/Career Advisor at Olympic High School, a large continuation school for at-risk teens in Concord, California. The new school year was about to begin, and my mind was engrossed in plans for the fall semester. The buzz from the phone gave me a start. It was my father-in-law.

"Hi, Dad. What's up?"

"Jenna is in foster care in Antioch. All three kids have been taken from Crystal. I'm not sure why, but I wonder if you would go find out."

I sat up. My heart sank.

"When did this happen?"

"Three days ago, I think. A woman from Social Services called me. Will you talk to her?"

I called my husband, Ric, first and told him what was happening. After a short conversation with Social Services, I jumped up from my desk, hurried to the office to tell the office manager where I was going, and drove my red Miata twenty minutes to the Social Services Department in Pittsburg. While I drove, I began to seethe. *This was just like Dad,* I thought, *always passive. Don't do anything; just sit and worry.* He drove me crazy with what I called Bonner Blinders. Ric and his three brothers wore them too. Rather than deal with situations, it was a lot easier to pretend they didn't exist or wish them away. Ric's mother had begun showing symptoms of dementia ten years earlier when she was sixty, yet none of them would admit there was a problem. "Oh, Mom's always been like this," they said. Now she was in advanced stages of Alzheimer's. I looked at my speedometer and backed off the gas pedal.

The case worker, Sharon, met me in the lobby and took me to her cubicle in the large office in Pittsburg. I explained to her that I was Jenna's aunt by marriage.

"Please tell me what you know about her situation," said Sharon.

"Jenna is seven, almost eight. She has been

abused and neglected her whole life. Her father is my husband Ric's brother Mark. We weren't able to report her mother because we never saw the cruelty in person, but we knew about it from my in-laws and our daughter Annie, who spent a lot of time with Jenna at their grandparents' home. Ric and I have often talked with Annie and our older daughter, Sara, about having Jenna come live with us. We are all in agreement that she deserves a happy, healthy life away from her mother.

"From infancy, she was with her mother about half the time and the other half with Ric's parents. They adore her and do everything they can to stay in her life. Her mother, Crystal, has virtually blackmailed them with statements like 'If you don't pay my electric bill, you won't see Jenna again," or "I'm out of groceries. Take me shopping.'

"My in-laws have taken care of Jenna whenever Crystal asked. She might stay with them for five hours or ten days; they never know how long it will be before Crystal reappears. Jenna always goes home with a supply of new clothes they never see again. Ric's parents love Jenna, but Mom has early-onset Alzheimer's, and Dad is overwhelmed.

"Jenna has two half-siblings; each has a different father. Brandon is four years younger than Jenna. His father has been with the family longest, but from what we know, he is a violent methamphetamine addict and dealer. Leticia is an infant. Her father was a one-night stand.

"I have tried for years to see if we could rescue Jenna. After fruitless phone calls and inquiries, I finally gave up. I learned that unless it's proven a child is physically abused or undeniably neglected, it's impossible to get the child away from the parents."

"That's pretty much true," said Sharon. "What about her father?"

"I'm sorry to be blunt," I said, "but Mark is absolutely worthless. He began using drugs in junior high school and has been in and out of my in-laws' house for years. He has rarely been part of Jenna's life."

Sharon asked me questions about Ric and our family, and me. She looked directly into my eyes. "I'm very glad you contacted me," she said. "Jenna needs to be in a better environment for the time being. Will you consider being her foster parents?"

I was prepared to do battle to keep Jenna with us forever. "That's why I'm here."

My mind reeled as Sharon told me what had happened. Jenna and her two half-siblings were taken from their mother when paramedics discovered the youngest, Leticia, had a broken arm. Her mom had left the three-month-old baby and

Brandon with a neighbor. When the neighbor noticed the baby's limp arm, she called 911. After investigating the situation, paramedics transferred the children to Social Services. A worker from Child Protective Services then took Jenna from her school.

Those other two poor kids. I hoped relatives of Jenna's half-siblings would care for them. Three children would be too much for us.

Sharon and I left her office and drove east in separate cars into an older neighborhood in Antioch. The homes there were small suburban boxes, likely built in the 1960s when the area's housing boom was at its height. Now, new homes were large and located in the hills above the old town. Front yards here were mostly barren, lawns dead and chock-full of dry weeds. I guessed most were rentals.

Sharon pulled her car over to the curb in front of a tan stucco house, and I parked behind her. We walked to the door. Dead chrysanthemums stuck out of two ceramic pots. Sharon knocked. I heard a baby crying inside. We waited. Three deadbolts were systematically unlocked, and the door opened. A thin, elderly black woman, stooped and more wrinkled than anyone I had ever seen, peered at us. I looked over her shoulder into Jenna's dark brown eyes. She was jumping, trying to see who was at the door.

"Aunt Alice, it's you!"

I eased by the two women and grabbed Jenna, hugging her tightly. "I'm here to take you to our house, Jenna." She did not let go of me.

While Sharon and the woman talked, I looked around the living room. There were no pictures on the walls, and a small, ragged couch was the single piece of furniture. The carpet was worn and stained. The scent of urine burned my nostrils. I looked to my right into a space that was probably meant to be a dining room. Three girls, two in diapers, sat on the floor in front of a small TV. In a crib against the rear wall a baby was crying. I was dismayed.

"Sharon," I said, "can I take Jenna now?" As I turned back to the door, with Jenna still hanging on to me, I asked my niece, "Where are your things?"

"The man who took me from school gave me a backpack." She ran to the back of the house and returned with a Spider-Man bag. I looked inside. There were a small stuffed bear, a pair of underpants, a T-shirt, and a pair of shorts.

"This is it?" She nodded. I took her hand and left the house. I couldn't wait to get Jenna home.

As I drove west on Highway 4, I felt giddy with success. I was thrilled with the opportunity to give Jenna a chance to live a wholesome, peaceful childhood. I was certain we could make her part of our family and raise her to be a loving, self-confident person. I turned to Jenna and said, "You can call me Mom if you want to."

Jenna looked at me. "You're not my mom. When am I going home?"

I could have kicked myself. Who was I to tell her I could be her mom? She had to be scared to death. It was ridiculous to think she knew what was going on. I focused, trying to think of a simple way to explain. "I'm so sorry, Jenna. You don't know anything about what happened the day you were picked up from school, do you?"

She shook her little head, tears forming in her eyes.

"First of all, know that I love you. You're going to stay with us for a while. Your mom left Leticia and Brandon with a neighbor that day, and she noticed Leticia's arm was injured. Do you know anything about that?" She stared at the floor. Her dark hair hid her face.

I continued. "Because your mom wasn't around, the neighbor called 911 and an ambulance took your sister to the hospital. Both she and Brandon are in foster homes like you were. I'm so happy I was able to bring you to our house until everything can get straightened out. I don't know how long you will stay with us."

Jenna lifted her head and turned toward the window. I put my hand around her shoulder. She flinched and stiffened. I patted her and replaced my hand on the steering wheel.

Keeping Jenna from ever going back to her mother was my goal. As much as I disliked Crystal, I told myself I must never say anything bad about her in front of Jenna. Down the road, when she understood how awful her situation had been, I hoped she would want us to adopt her.

Looking back now, some twenty years later, I am amazed at how little I had prepared myself for what was to come.

2

Jenna's New Home

As I drove home with Jenna next to me, her small, round body was tucked into my sports car's passenger seat. She had dark skin and short, straight brown hair from her mother's Mexican heritage, and she was a bit overweight, a Bonner trait. Her eyes were so nearly black they seemed to have no pupils. Thrilled to give her the opportunity of a safe, warm family environment, I resolved to keep her from returning to Crystal.

I laughed inside. One day years earlier, when Sara was five and Annie, two, I had stood at the kitchen sink contemplating my life. The girls were wonderful, but they certainly weren't the three-boy family I'd envisioned when I was young. If I had a third child, I thought, it would undoubtedly be another girl. Two was fine: room between them in the back seat of the car, one for each of us to handle. Now I had three daughters after all. Funny.

Along the way, Jenna told me what happened. "This man came up to me at recess and said to come with him. He took me to the lady's house where you picked me up. But he lied. He told me I would be back with my mom in a couple of days. I hate that man."

"How long were you at the lady's house?"

"At least a week. I was so excited to see you when you came to get me, Aunt Alice. I thought I was going to be stuck there forever. That lady was mean. She made me and the other girls sit in the room all day. We didn't do anything but watch TV."

The timing didn't match what Dad thought, but I couldn't trust him. He was oblivious amid his efforts to cope with Mom's Alzheimer's, Mark's drug problems, Crystal's blackmailing, and Jenna's dreadful life. The social worker had told me the kids were removed from their mom five days ago. I would have to ask her for more details.

We slowed to a stop at the Alhambra Avenue exit, turned left under the highway and Santa Fe Railroad trestle, drove through wooded Alhambra Valley, and went up steep Sage Drive to our house.

Jenna had visited our home many times and was particularly close to Annie, who would begin her senior year in high school the following week. Sara lived in a Daly City apartment and was a junior majoring in psychology at San Francisco State University. She often came home on weekends. Jenna idolized her cousins.

As I drove up our driveway, I thought what a radical change this home would be for Jenna. She had been to our house for dinners, birthday parties, and holidays, so she was familiar with it. But living here? For all her seven years, she had been passed between ghetto apartments in Antioch with her mom and the suburban, enabling home of my in-laws in Concord. That was what she knew.

Her life was entirely different from ours. Ric and I had both grown up in families of four children with professional fathers and stay-at-home moms. We did well in school. College was a given. We met at UC Davis, got married in 1974 shortly after graduation, and rented a small house in Martinez, a fifteen-minute drive from Ric's job as a chemical engineer at an oil refinery. I played housewife for nine months before I found a job writing environmental impact reports at the Contra Costa County Planning Department. We used birth control, saved all my salary, and bought our first home two years later. Sara was born two years after that. Shortly before Annie came along in 1981, we moved to a three-bedroom, ranch-style house. When Annie was five, I began to yearn for a larger, more unique home.

When we married, Ric and I made a pact: he would retire as early as possible from the refinery and we'd move to the woods. I had majored in wildlife biology, and during two college summers we lived and worked in the Sierras north of Lake Tahoe with a group of friends. I loved it there. Living in a small community in the mountains was my ultimate dream. "All I want is a cabin in the woods" became my mantra.

I had to wait twenty more years for that, but I was determined to find something as close to it as possible in the interim. I searched with our realtor for a full year. Then one day we drove up a long, circular driveway. We couldn't see the house for all the trees until we reached the top.

"This is it," I said to him. "I don't even care what it looks like inside. This is the place." The three-story house was set at the back corner of an acre, hidden behind a mass of trees. Oak-covered hills within a 6,000-acre public open space area lay directly behind the property. The house resembled a Tahoe cabin, with rustic wood paneling and a loft next to the master bedroom. The views were spectacular. Mt. Diablo loomed in the distance to the east, Briones Regional Park took up the entire southerly view, and tall pine trees grew outside the bedroom windows. This was as close to the woods as I was ever going to get in Martinez.

The day I brought Jenna home we had lived at the Sage Drive house for eleven years. During that time, we remodeled the kitchen, updated the pool, added landscaping, and planted a huge vegetable garden. I was surprised when, in their teenage years, both Sara and Annie told me they were embarrassed about living there. It was too fancy for them, too rich, too different from the homes of their friends. It was a unique home in suburbia, but to me it was simply a placeholder where we could raise our family before moving to the woods. To Jenna, it must have been a mansion.

We parked, walked under our rose-laden trellis, and climbed the stairs to the house. As we entered the kitchen, I said, "You can have Annie's old room, Jenna. When Sara moved to San Francisco, Annie decided to take over her room with the double bed. I actually like her old room better. It has that big desk with all the drawers and shelves and cabinets above it. The woman who lived here before we bought the house used it for her graphic design business."

I was babbling. Poor Jenna. She must be so confused and scared. I sat on the bed and patted the bedspread beside me. She sat down.

"This must be awfully hard for you. Are you scared?"

She nodded.

"You're safe now, Jenna. We love you and want you to stay with us. I don't know what's going to happen with your mom, but as soon as I find out I'll let you know. I'll also find out where Brandon and Leticia are so you can see them as soon as possible." I gave her a big hug. She was limp and didn't react. I stood up.

"I bet you're hungry. Do you want something to eat? Dinnertime is a long way off. Uncle Ric usually doesn't get home until about six-thirty, so we eat late. I think a snack is just what the doctor ordered."

She followed me into the kitchen.

"How about a tuna sandwich?"

"All right. I like tuna fish."

As I got out a can of Starkist, mayonnaise, pickle relish, and bread, I thought about my mom's tuna sandwiches. My childhood had been a Beaver Cleaver life. Jenna didn't even know who Beaver was and had no experience with a life like his. The sandwich was on the cutting board. I turned and reached up to get a plate from the cupboard. When I looked back, Jenna was eating the sandwich over the sink.

"Jenna, take this and eat your sandwich at the table."

She gave me a sidelong, serious look. "Aunt Alice, a lot of people eat like this."

3

Before the Rescue

Ric was the oldest of four boys. Jenna's father, Mark, the third son, was fourteen years younger than Ric. Mark had been a happy kid who loved sports and did well in school until eighth grade, when he began to get into trouble. Although very intelligent, he was a smartass who always thought he had a better idea. We knew there were problems, but Mom and Dad were vague about details. We didn't press, because our own children were our focus. Sara was born when Mark was fifteen.

Mark had a wonderful girlfriend his sophomore year in high school. Kim was cute with long, wavy brown hair. Sara adored her, and Kim paid special attention to Sara. She would sit our toddler on Mom's vanity and make her beautiful with a little mascara and lipstick, and hair ribbons. She and Mark often took Sara on picnics and to the mall. Kim made him a better person; he was kinder, less self-absorbed.

Then at the end of the school year, Kim's father was transferred to the east coast. Her leaving caused Mark to spiral down. He got kicked off the football team early in the fall. He was sullen and short-tempered at home. Mom called him a "street angel, home devil." Even so, he took the SAT college entrance exams and must have had very high scores, as reams of brochures came to him in the mail. Rather than go to a university, however, after graduation he chose to attend Diablo Valley Community College and work at RadioShack. He dropped out of school after less than a year.

Jackie was his next girlfriend. Cuss words flowed freely from her mouth, she wore tight dresses, and she crudely slathered makeup on her face. She looked like a street whore—a far cry from sweet Kim. After Jackie, Mark began to disappear for days and return in a foul mood.

Annie was visiting one Saturday when Mark stormed into the house, yelling. He turned, kicked the front door open, and threw something into the street. From what Annie told us, it was likely a drug paraphernalia kit.

When Mark was twenty-six, the year before Jenna was born, his drug use was rampant. Mom and Dad gave him money and allowed him to maintain a bedroom in their home. It was extremely frustrating that they would not draw the line with him. Tough love was not in their nature.

Jenna's life began as a lie. Mark told his parents his new girlfriend, Crystal, was pregnant and needed a place to stay. My in-laws felt sorry for her and allowed the couple to live with them. Fast-forward several months: Crystal hadn't been pregnant then but became so after she established residency in Mom and Dad's comfortable home. She slithered into their lives like a venomous snake. She told them she had no family, but later we found out her parents had kicked her out at sixteen. She went from them to Mark, and then to Mom and Dad. The couple said they had been married in Reno. We never knew if that was true or not.

I first met Crystal when I dropped by Mom and Dad's house while I was in the neighborhood. Mom answered the door in curlers and a housecoat, her usual attire at home. Walking down the hallway toward the door was a young woman wearing Mom's bathrobe and slippers. Her long, dark brown hair was unkempt. Acne spread across her face. She glanced at me, yawned, and continued towards the galley kitchen.

"Crystal, come meet Alice, Ric's wife."

She turned toward me but didn't look me in the eye. "Hullo," she said. Giving me the slightest of nods, she continued into the kitchen. I already knew a little about the situation, and even as low-life as Mark had become, it was hard to see what he saw in Crystal.

Mom looked at me. "Crystal is staying with us for a while until she can find another place to live." Crystal shuffled to the refrigerator, peered into it, gave me a sidelong look, and smirked. I was not impressed.

Mark worked full time at RadioShack. How he was able to maintain a job was a mystery, and perhaps another lie. Mom and Dad tried to treat Crystal like a daughter, but she was an extremely difficult person to live with. She complained constantly and didn't help out around the house. She acted like they owed her a leisurely life. She made no attempt to get a job. Early on they bought her a bicycle and encouraged her to attend the nearby adult school to get her GED. She quit after two weeks. When she became pregnant, Mom doted on her. She made sure she got prenatal care and served her nutritious food. Her dementia didn't keep her from what she knew best, motherhood.

I overheard Crystal talking to a friend, also pregnant, at the wedding of Ric's youngest brother, Andrew. Reclining on a lounge chair by the venue's pool and behind blue-glazed sunglasses, she twisted her huge belly, leaned over, and said to her friend, "You know, I got pregnant so I could get money from the county. Now it looks like I won't need it after all." Her friend laughed. At that time, single mothers qualified for General Assistance from the government. Her comment sickened me.

Ric's parents were at the hospital when Jenna was born in September 1990. As grandparents do, they fell in love with her. She lived at their house with Mark and Crystal for three months, but when their behavior became too much to endure—they got into massive, blowout fights and came and went as they pleased—Mom and Dad rented an apartment in Antioch for the three of them, hoping Mark and Crystal would take responsibility for their child. Soon after, Mark moved out of the apartment and disappeared. Even though he was gone, Crystal knew she had a cash cow and took total advantage of my in-laws. By blackmailing them with Jenna, she had free food, a place to live, and at-the-ready babysitters.

Ric and I were dismayed by the situation, but we were unable to talk sense into Mom and Dad.

They would do anything to protect Jenna. Crystal became pregnant from another man when Jenna was three. Mark came home occasionally, but he wasn't involved with Crystal or Jenna.

I was at the house one day when Mark came through the front door. Jenna ran to him, clinging to his legs and looking up at him, calling, "Daddy, Daddy." He patted her head and said, "Hi, Jenna." Nothing more. His drug use became worse; at one point he nailed his bedroom door shut from the inside and crawled in and out through the window.

Jenna could not have had a more confusing life. She spent half her time with her mother, where she was surrounded by drug use and violence. We didn't know the details of her abuse and squalid living conditions, but we assumed the worst. She was with Mom and Dad when she wasn't with Crystal. They gave her whatever she wanted and showered her with love. Complete power in one place, none in the other.

Symptoms of Mom's Alzheimer's, forgetfulness and confusion, began in 1988 when she was sixty years old and two years before Jenna was born. I recognized her idiosyncrasies early on, but Ric, his brothers, and their dad insisted, "She has always been like this." That's when I coined the phrase Bonner Blinders. Ignoring the changes in her was easier for them. But getting lost driving familiar streets in her neighborhood and leaving her purse in the refrigerator were not normal. There was something wrong with a person who plastered hundreds of phone numbers and notes all over her utility room cabinets.

Dad wouldn't take her to a doctor because "she doesn't want to go." I brought him educational materials about Alzheimer's and dementia. He ignored them. I was torn: I was the daughter-in-law, not the daughter. Her family should be dealing with this. If she were my mother I would carry her to a doctor if I had to. Ric worked fifty to sixty hours a week, and I couldn't budge him. Andrew, the youngest son, was newly married, and John, five and a half years younger than Ric, lived in Davis with his wife and two small children. I was the one who had the time and fortitude.

I became desperate when it was obvious Mom wasn't bathing. Her hair was stringy and her body odor, rank. Dad said, "I can't get her to take a shower." I finally convinced him to make an appointment with a geriatric specialist, but it was I who took her there. The doctor asked her simple questions. She didn't know who our president was and was unsure of the day of the week or the present year. After a short time the doctor told us she likely had Alzheimer's. Mom didn't react except to say, "Oh, dear." As it happened, she declined over fourteen years, passing when she was seventy-four.

My friend Georgia's mother had lived with the same terrible disease for several years. After she died, Georgia was compelled to make a difference for people with dementia. She secured funding and started a day care program so caregivers could have some free time and their loved ones would enjoy stimulation like dancing and games. She also maintained a resource center. I persuaded Dad to meet her, and she suggested Dad hire hourly help from a roster of qualified home care professionals. They would assist with bathing, make meals, and spend time with Mom. He was finally ready.

By this time Jenna was a little girl. During kindergarten and first grade, she was absent more than fifty days each year. She told me later she had to walk herself to school most days. In second grade she lived with Mom and Dad during the week and attended a nearby elementary school. She was with her mother on weekends. Crystal called when she knew social workers were coming for a visit. She needed Jenna with her at those times so she could qualify for maximum General Assistance.

As Mom's Alzheimer's worsened, she began

to act like a child herself; she and Jenna often fought like siblings. Fortunately, Dad wouldn't allow Crystal to drop toddler Brandon off along with Jenna. He had enough to deal with.

Although we frequently saw Jenna when we visited Mom and Dad, our daughter Annie was most familiar with Jenna's day-to-day circumstances. Annie spent considerable time with her grandparents. In addition to playing with Jenna, she often drove with Dad to Crystal's apartment. Annie was terribly concerned about Jenna and the kinds of people Crystal hung out with. Once, when Jenna was six, Annie attended her birthday party in a park. She received a cute puppy from her mother. The next time Annie saw Jenna and asked about her puppy, she said, "Alan (Brandon's father) got mad and threw him over our apartment railing. He died." All of us were appalled by the story.

Welfare-to-Work legislation was enacted in 1996. The popular program was to "end welfare as we have come to know it," said President Clinton. Welfare recipients were now required to work or receive job training. Crystal became my litmus test. Would the system really be able to push her off the government gravy train and turn her into a productive citizen? The old joke about selling the Brooklyn Bridge was easier to swallow.

Three years later a student at Olympic, the

high school where I worked, stopped me in the hall one day.

"You're raising a little girl named Jenna, aren't you?"

My eyebrows scrunched and I tilted my head. "I am. How did you know?"

"I work with her mother at Kmart." She gave me a serious look. "I'm very glad Jenna is with you."

She kept walking and said no more. She didn't need to. As far as I knew, that was the only job Crystal had ever had, and it didn't last. Even if she no longer received government assistance, I was certain she would find a way to survive on her own with Mom and Dad's help … or with men she happened to be with.

In March 1998, six months before we rescued Jenna, Ric and I dropped by Mom and Dad's to visit. We were furious to find Crystal, pregnant once more, living there with Jenna and Brandon. When she saw us, she pushed the kids down the hallway and into a back bedroom.

Ric said, "Dad, what in the hell are you thinking?"

"Crystal got evicted and had no place to go," said Dad. "It's only temporary."

"Having her live with you is no solution. You know that. You have too much on your plate already, dealing with Mom, Mark, Jenna, and

Crystal. You can bet Crystal won't find a new place. Why should she when you give in to her every whim?" Veins were bulging on Ric's temples. I put my hand on his arm.

Ric and his dad had a unique relationship. Dad had great respect for Ric. Before his retirement, Dad had been a successful refinery engineer like Ric. They enjoyed talking shop when they were together. When Mark began getting into trouble in junior high, Ric told Dad he should be firm with Mark. But nothing changed. Dad avoided confrontation at all costs. I'd likened him to a floating helium balloon, bouncing one way, then another, never getting anywhere. As the years went on, it became common that Ric lectured and Dad nodded and then ignored him—his own style of passive-aggressive behavior. On this particular day, when we found Crystal and her kids at their house, Dad stood silently as we took charge and moved them to a nearby motel.

We paid for two nights and gave her fifty dollars. Crystal feared Ric because he was stern, and she knew he meant what he said. She also feared me because I knew many people who worked for the system that funded her lifestyle, politicians as well as employees of the county government. We went back to Mom and Dad's, gathered the rest of Crystal's things, and returned to the motel. The kids were playing with newly purchased cheap toys, and a huge pizza box was on the bed. So much for the fifty dollars. As we left, Ric turned to Crystal. "Do not go back to my parents' house." She neither met his eyes nor responded.

After that, our family talked seriously about having Jenna come live with us. Sara was nineteen, Annie, sixteen. Ric and I were in our late forties. We knew it would be challenging, but she was a little girl who deserved to have some stability in her life. I felt empowered to be her would-be savior. I contacted several acquaintances in the foster care and social services community to seek their advice. Each one told me the process would be difficult, but it wasn't until I called Child Protective Services that I became truly discouraged. Even though we knew Jenna was suffering from an abusive, horrific situation, we had no way to prove it.

Six months later the situation resolved itself without our doing anything. Crystal abandoned her injured baby, and the children were taken to foster homes.

4

Sourdough Pancakes

Sitting next to Jenna on her bed, I put down *Charlotte's Web* and said to her, "Tomorrow you'll have a special treat for breakfast. I'll tell you about it in the morning."

"Why not now?"

"I want to keep it a surprise. I think you'll love it." I leaned over and gave her a goodnight kiss. She lay still.

As soon as she moved in, we tried to make Jenna feel like she was an integral part of our family. I love traditions. The things we do at Christmas, Easter, Thanksgiving, and family reunions warm my heart. Every Sunday we made a special breakfast: sourdough pancakes and bacon. In 1978, shortly after Sara was born, one of our best friends sent us a present from Alaska where he worked as a bush pilot. The gift came carefully wrapped in bubble plastic and foam peanuts. Inside was a brown-and-blue pottery crock, obviously handmade. Tucked in the crock was a plastic bag filled with white goop. A short letter and notecard explained.

> Merry Christmas Ric, Alice, and Sara. This is sourdough starter that originated in the Alaskan Gold Rush, or so I was told. Store it in the crock, never glass. Keep it in the refrigerator until you are ready to use it. You can make bread, but my favorite is pancakes. They're delicious and easy. Enclosed is the recipe. Miss you guys. Love, Tom.

On a three by five card was the recipe I still use more than forty years later.

Tom's Sourdough Pancakes (serves 3–4)

The night before, stir together 1/2 C starter, 1 C hot tap water, and 1 C flour. Leave the bowl out at room temperature. In the morning, the mixture should be thick and bubbly. Refill the crock. To the rest, add a mixture of 2 eggs and 2 Tbl vegetable oil, beaten. Just before you're ready to make pancakes, mix 1 tsp baking soda, 1 tsp baking powder, and 2 Tbl sugar with a little water and add them to the batter. The recipe is easily halved or multiplied depending on the number of eaters and their appetites. (If you don't use the starter for a while it will separate and turn gray. No worries. Just "exercise" it by making the starter–hot water–flour mixture one or two nights in a row. It's very forgiving. Remember, the miners used to sleep with it at night.)

Over the years, there was rarely a Sunday without sourdough pancakes. We took the starter camping and on vacations. I learned to store it in a lidded container inside a Ziploc bag when we traveled. Otherwise, if we were at high altitudes it would expand and pop the top, creating a mushy mess. Everyone loved the pancakes. They were light and thin, almost like crepes. The girls favored Log Cabin syrup, but Ric and I learned to love real maple after my cousin Jane gave us syrup her family made from their own trees in northern Minnesota. We grew boysenberries in our garden, and I discovered a way to make berry syrup using my usual jam recipe without pectin, and a food mill to eliminate the seeds. Delicious.

We enjoyed serving our special treat to family and friends. We especially liked sharing the starter. My mom and dad loved them as much as we did. When my mother developed severe food allergies, she substituted rice flour for wheat. They came out a little crispy but she could eat them without prickly rashes, and they tasted good. Our friends Bud and Lois used the starter for years in their Alabama bed and breakfast inn. Their guests loved hearing about the starter's history. Most people forgot to use it after a while and eventually threw it out, but we were always willing to resupply them if they wanted to try again. We came close to losing our batch several times, particularly after the girls left home and we stopped making them weekly. Once, it grew a thick layer of white mold. I scraped it off and exercised it a few times until it looked happy again. I took Tom's words, "It's very forgiving," to heart.

The first Sunday Jenna lived with us, Sara, Annie, Ric, and I couldn't wait to include her in our tradition. We told her the story, one on top of the other, laughing as we set the table, fried the bacon, mixed the batter, and started flipping. Jenna didn't say anything until the first pancakes went into the oven to keep them warm. "I think I'd rather have cereal," she said.

"Why, Jenna?" I asked. "You'll love them, I'm sure." She looked at me with a steady gaze. "At least try them. If you really don't like them, you don't have to eat them."

The family banter ceased. After I put the heaping platter on the table, I placed one pancake on her plate and moved the butter and syrup in front of her.

Jenna spread butter on the pancake, dribbled some syrup, and cut a small bite. She immediately spit it out. Screwing up her face, she said, "I'd rather have cereal."

5

Going Crazy

The year before Jenna came to live with us, I was in my third year at Olympic High School working as the College/Career Advisor. An alternative school for potential dropouts, Olympic was large, with some 300 sixteen-to eighteen-year-olds enrolled.

My job description was uniquely open ended. I focused on college, military, apprenticeships, and job skills. I exposed our at-risk students to professional community members and post–high school opportunities as often as I could. With my principal's approval, I had the freedom to try whatever I thought might engage our students, who had been disenfranchised from school for years. I wore many hats: I ran the Career Center, taught a job skills class, and held biweekly orientations for new students. I also recruited speakers and took groups of kids on field trips to businesses and colleges. I loved being on the go, connecting with people all over the county.

In the fall I began losing weight without trying. I had fought excess weight since I was a kid, so this was brand new. Even though I was hungrier and ate more than usual, I continued to lose weight. I loved the new me, especially when friends complimented me with "You look wonderful." I went to Kaiser Permanente in January to have a regular physical and blood work. A day later a nurse called.

"Have you been losing weight?"

"Yes, I have. Why do you ask?"

"Have you had trouble sleeping?"

"Actually, I've had a terrible time sleeping lately. Why?"

"When you lean over, do you feel a jerking sensation in your body?"

"Now you've really got me worried. I've noticed that very thing lately when I bend down to get the laundry out of the dryer. What in the world is wrong with me?"

"The blood tests show you have an overactive thyroid, or Graves' disease. You need to come see your doctor right away."

As much as I loved losing weight, I learned that a hyperactive thyroid can be very dangerous, weakening muscles and other organs in the body. Damn—the one time in my life when I didn't have to worry about what I ate, and my health was at risk because of it. After consultations with my regular doctor and an endocrinologist, we decided I would take a drug that would mask the symptoms and see what happened. I figured since the condition came on suddenly, it might just as quickly disappear. But after six months, my metabolism was still out of whack. My doctors recommended I have my thyroid treated with radioactive iodine, a common procedure. The treatment would gradually shrink the gland, ultimately destroying it. I would need to take thyroid replacement hormones for the rest of my life. It worked, and my sleeplessness disappeared.

Two days after I rescued Jenna, I pulled up to the curb in my little red Miata and walked into the main office of Olympic. Ric and I had been in juvenile court most of the morning; my thoughts weren't on my job. We were now officially foster parents. School started the following week.

Marcie, the principal, saw me as I walked in. "Oh, I'm so glad you're back. Come in." She shut the door. Marcie had an open-door policy, so I knew she wanted to talk to me about something confidential. Before I could sit down, Marcie said,

"Lila called this morning, and she's not coming back. I want you to take over her classroom for the year. I know you can do it. You're familiar with the curriculum, and you've already started your credential program. You'll be a great teacher. It'll be easy to get an emergency credential."

The previous spring I had begun a two-year teaching credential program at a local university, taking classes at night and on weekends. My goal was to work with teachers to improve student learning. I didn't think I was well suited to the classroom and had no intention of giving up my position, but I thought I would gain respect from other teachers and learn a lot.

I dropped into a chair, clasped my hands, and stared at the floor. I respected Marcie and would do just about anything for her and the students at Olympic, but I knew I wasn't ready to teach. I raised my eyes and looked into hers.

"I really need you, Alice."

"What about the Service Learning Academy?" Three teachers and I had worked all summer to create a unique program in which students could earn required credits while volunteering in the community. We had designed curriculum and defined our roles. I was to be the point person since I could easily change my daily schedule. We were ready to accept students.

"I've already talked with the team. We'll have to cancel the program."

I was devastated. This new opportunity for students was exciting and challenging—all our work, for nothing. My brain churned for a few seconds longer. I took a deep breath and sighed. "Well, I've just begun one life change, why not take on another?"

I had no idea how those words would come back to haunt me.

Jeanette, the teacher who had created the class I was to teach, Economics for Everyday Living, had been creative and effective. Originally designed for home economics, her room had three separate kitchen areas and a ton of storage. Jeanette had built a superb program over a dozen years and had also co-written a popular textbook for hands-on math. Her file cabinets were filled with unique, interesting curriculum for our at-risk students. Each day she greeted them at the door with play-money income, their reward for coming to class on time. They used simulated checking and savings accounts and balanced monthly statements. They cut ads out of newspapers, called rental agents, cooked meals, and calculated differences in costs between cloth and disposable diapers, fast food and home-cooked meals, and new and second-hand furniture. I was very familiar with her program, but I was certain I couldn't do a good job as a teacher there. I lacked skills and confidence—the reasons I hadn't gone into teaching in the first place. I didn't think I had what it took to be effective, and I did not want to be like one of the many poor teachers I had known.

Unfortunately, Jeanette had retired the previous year, and Lila, the teacher hired to replace her, had literally destroyed the program. Scattered, ill-prepared, and incompetent, she was the kind of teacher I feared I might be. In June, Marcie had encouraged her to seek other employment.

Lila had left the classroom in shambles. There were unorganized stacks of lessons and material everywhere. Jeanette's carefully marked kitchen utensils were all over the room. The stacked file cabinets were half empty and disorganized.

On Thursday, the day after Jenna came home with me, I registered her at John Swett Elementary School and enrolled her in their after-school day care program. On Friday Marcie told me I had a new job. On Monday I dropped Jenna off at school, drove to Olympic, and walked into my classroom, petrified. This was not going to be good.

Fortunately, due to the nature of our at-risk students, who disliked school and had little motivation, few of them showed up the first week.

Those who did helped me clean up and reorganize the room. Once it was set up, I hoped I would be ready to teach, but I wasn't. I felt incompetent.

Taking classes at night and trying to teach for the first time took its toll. And now there was Jenna to worry about. At eight years old she lacked many social skills: she grabbed and gobbled food from the dinner table, didn't use a napkin, constantly interrupted conversations, hadn't been taught to say please and thank you, and rarely changed her underwear. Bath times were particularly frustrating. She was too old for me to be directly in charge of her bathing, but she didn't use shampoo despite my instructions. Her thick hair was oily and matted.

I tried my best to help her make up for those lost aspects of parental guidance, but she resented my interference. At her mother's house she was left on her own, and Mom and Dad Bonner felt so sorry for her that they let her behave as she wanted.

I began to have trouble sleeping. I had suffered from occasional insomnia since I was in my early twenties. Most recently Graves' disease was the culprit. Now it was much worse. Periodically I fell asleep easily but awoke shortly after midnight, thoughts swirling in my head. Reading seemed to calm my monkey brain and allow me to resume sleeping. Occasionally I had a full night's rest, but more often I'd read, sleep for a few minutes, wake up, worry, read, sleep, and continue the pattern. Ric got very tired of hearing the click of the reading lamp. Days went by when I had to get by on two to three hours of sleep a night. Words seemed to fly by me. I couldn't focus.

I thought perhaps my thyroid levels had increased, but that wasn't the cause; my levels were normal. The problem went on for weeks. I tried home remedies. I drank warm milk and took baths before bed. I took melatonin. I wrote down all the things I might worry about so I could put them out of my mind. I had several sessions of hypnotherapy. Nothing worked. After six weeks I was a wreck, and I knew I needed more help.

Since childhood I had worked through problems by myself. I was a strong person; I could handle any obstacle. It was difficult for me to seek professional help. Finally, however, I made an appointment to see a therapist at Kaiser Permanente.

I was reading a magazine in a small waiting area when a woman about my age called my name. She had permed blond hair and wore a blue wool suit. Joyce introduced herself and led me to her office. It was small and dark. The single window was covered by a flowered curtain. A desk was littered with file folders. Lavender perfumed the air. I sat next to a table that held a lamp and a box of tissues. *Oh no,* I thought. *I hope I don't need that tissue.* I wanted to learn how to sleep, not break down in tears. Joyce pulled out a new pad of yellow paper and asked me why I was there.

She was kind and a good listener. Through talk therapy, she and I discovered my bouts of sleeplessness happened during times of stress related to work. Not necessarily paid work; for years I'd been a nearly full-time volunteer in our community. I told her about specific times I could remember: when I was in charge of the summer day camp for Camp Fire Girls and Boys; served as PTA president and school board president; developed and coordinated a countywide school volunteer program; wrote and published environmental impact reports. Whenever I felt I wasn't living up to my own expectations, I'd worry through the night. Come daytime I'd realize how ridiculous my concerns were and go about my day.

After two sessions Joyce suggested a possible cause related to my upbringing. My parents couldn't have been more stable or loving, but they never, ever said those three so-important words. I knew they loved me; they showed it all the time. Perhaps my need to push myself to do more, more, more was an attempt to capture my parents' attention, Joyce said.

Unfortunately, understanding that deep need wasn't enough. I still couldn't sleep. Joyce referred me to a psychiatrist who prescribed drugs to alleviate my insomnia. None of them worked. My days were like a fuzzy dream; I couldn't focus on the simplest chore or conversation.

My family did their best to support me. Ric cut back his over-the-top hours at work and made sure he was home evenings to help with Jenna. Annie filled in when she could. On weekends, Sara often came home from college to give me some relief.

At the same time, my brother was experiencing sleeping problems as well. He recommended I try a sleep aid called Restoril. Restoril … just the sound of it was calming. My primary doctor prescribed it for me, but he warned me the drug could become habit forming; I should use it sparingly. The very first night I was amazed at the result. I slept soundly for six hours: no dreams, no waking up, just dead sleep.

My physician father had considered minor health problems insignificant when my siblings and I were kids. If we complained, Dad retorted with his favorite saying: "Ten years from now you'll forget all about it." I learned to avoid talking about ailments. It was hard for me to bring up my sleep issue, but one day I mentioned it to Dad on the phone. He said, "Go ahead and take the sleeping pills if you need them. You'll be fine."

So I did. Night after night. I knew I shouldn't

take Restoril continuously, but it felt so good to sleep. Dad was eighty-seven. I loved him and he'd been an excellent doctor in his day, but I was certain that in this case he really didn't know what he was talking about.

During Christmas vacation I realized I was addicted to Restoril. I had to quit. I stopped taking the pills, and I was awake for three solid days. But I survived . . . and I climbed back on the sleeplessness train.

By February I was an absolute mess. One of the drugs the psychiatrist prescribed made me feel like a zombie. Another made my lips burn and caused my thoughts to swirl. My mouth was so dry with a third that I found it difficult to chew and swallow.

Work was no better. With Olympic's unique schedule, students were able to attend any of their five classes as often as they liked each day. With this flexibility, sometimes no kids came to class at all, and I'd find myself sitting, staring at my desk. Other times a few kids chose to come to my class, and I'd let them use whatever food items were in the refrigerator to cook for themselves. I couldn't focus.

As part of my teaching credential program, a supervisor from the university was assigned to mentor me and observe me teach. I was able to use my working position as half my student teaching for a semester and would teach at a different school in the fall. I was honest with her about my difficulties.

"You're not hurting any of your students, are you?" she asked.

"No, but I'm not teaching them much of anything either."

"You'll be fine. Soon things in your life will calm down and you'll be effective, I'm sure of it." I appreciated her reassurance, but I still doubted my abilities.

Finally, relief. The psychiatrist prescribed Paxil, a drug used to treat anxiety as opposed to insomnia. It took a month for it to take effect, but once it did, I began to sleep. And relax. And not worry. I was alive again. I felt like me.

6

Three Scoops

Jenna was not adapting any better to living with us. She rarely smiled, and having a two-way conversation with her was nearly impossible. She answered with single words or not at all. Staring at us with vacant eyes seemed to be her strength, her way of coping.

Her abuse manifested itself in telling ways. Once, I sent her to her room for talking back to me, the same consequence I had used with our daughters. As I attempted to shut the door, she dropped to the floor writhing, frothing at the mouth, and crying, "Don't lock me in, don't lock me in!"

Another time, Ric and I were in the kitchen,

face to face, arguing about something so inconse-
quential I have no memory of it. I vividly recall,
however, her small body squeezing in between
us, looking first at one of us, then the other. I
squatted down. "Jenna, this is as angry as you
will ever see us. We will never yell or scream at
one another." We both hugged her but she didn't
respond.

I knew I had to find a good counselor for
Jenna. She had been abused for her entire life and
needed to talk to a professional, someone other
than us. Three weeks after she came to live with
us, a friend who was a retired juvenile probation
officer suggested I call Grace McMahon. "I've
known her a long time, and I think she is a perfect
fit for Jenna. If she can't take any new clients,
I'm sure she can recommend another therapist,"
he said.

Jenna liked Grace right away, and so did I. She
was grandmotherly, with curly white hair, a face
full of soft folds, and a plump body. She shared
an old house with another therapist two blocks
from where I worked. Her office was decorated in
forties-style comfort. Two overstuffed chairs were
placed on either side of a plush Turkish rug. A
roll-top oak desk faced a picture window which
framed dense, green shrubbery. Against the rear
wall next to the door sat a flowered sofa. The scent
of jasmine filled the air. Once we were inside

the room, traffic and voices disappeared. It was a warm cocoon.

I spent a session with Grace before she met Jenna. She asked me probing questions about Jenna's trauma, and it was easy to share my feelings with her. As I left, I felt confident she was the right person to help our niece. Thereafter, every Wednesday I left my job thirty minutes early, drove to Martinez, picked up Jenna at John Swett Elementary, then backtracked to Grace's office. I snatched some time at my desk at Olympic while the two met. My principal, Marcie, understood; she allowed me to set my own time outside the hours when students were there.

Jenna seemed happy when I picked her up after each session. She especially liked it when Grace took her to the nearby ice cream store. I rarely had the opportunity to check on Jenna's progress, so one day I made an appointment to see Grace when Jenna was still in school. I sat down on her couch. Grace leaned forward in her chair. I spoke first.

"How is Jenna doing?'

"She's a hard nut to crack, Alice."

"Tell me about it. I often feel like we're living with an empty vessel."

"It's interesting you mention the word empty," said Grace. "You might have wondered why I've been taking her out for ice cream."

"You're right. I figured there was a reason for it, but I haven't had a chance to ask you about it."

"With children, I find they will more easily open up if we do something besides sit in my office. Has she told you we've been sewing?"

"She pretty much tells me nothing."

"We've been making Christmas ornaments from felt." Grace showed me a cute blue and pink bird that might hang on a tree. "She seems to enjoy cutting, pinning, and stitching." She paused. "There's something interesting about the ice cream I want to share with you. She always asks for three scoops. And she never finishes it."

"That's strange."

"Actually, it's very indicative of a child who has been neglected. Her mother rarely showed affection. Every time they moved, Jenna had to leave the few things she had behind. By asking for three scoops, she's trying to get as much as she can at the moment, whether she really wants it or not."

I thought for a moment. "That kind of makes sense, but it would be nice if she would allow us to provide her the love she craves. I know I'm not her mother, but she gives us absolutely nothing. No hugs, no 'I love you's.' It's all we can do to get her to smile.

"What's especially peculiar is that she makes friends so easily elsewhere. At a park she'll walk right up to another child and start a conversation. She has no fear of talking to strangers in stores like my kids did at her age. She doesn't have any trouble on the playground at school, although she tends to hang out with the yard supervisors."

Grace said, "That's also indicative of a neglected child. She's trying to find love wherever she can. Unfortunately, she can't allow herself to accept it from the one place she can easily get it, from you and your family. Jenna has been made to feel worthless for her entire life. She can't love herself. And until she does, she can't love you.

"There's another aspect I've noticed. She's what we call a parentified child. Because Crystal was on drugs, drunk, or gone, Jenna had to act as the mother of her brother and baby sister. She also had to take care of her own mother, reversing their relationship and placing a very heavy load on her shoulders. She is one mixed up, damaged little girl. Jenna has actually suffered more than any other child I have counseled."

"We've got a long way to go, don't we?"

"Yes, and she may never get there. All you can do is to continue what you're doing: provide her a safe, loving environment."

"I can do that, but she doesn't make it easy." I laughed. "Thank God I've got my own therapist."

I continued to see Joyce occasionally. When I told her about Jenna and our difficulties with her, she said, "You want to wave a magic wand and make her better, don't you?"

I thought a moment, looked at her, and nodded.

"Well, you can't. All you can do is provide a loving, stable family environment."

"That's the same advice Jenna's counselor gave me," I said, smiling, "and our whole family wants to give her that."

7

Lunch Money

Even though Jenna was an enormous challenge, and she wasn't a normal child, parenting her was relatively easy. We had already gone through all the trials of raising two girls: tantrums, whining, doldrums, puberty, anxiety, mean friends. Fortunately, we had skipped Jenna's baby years with the foul diapers and sleep deprivation. We had rules, standards, rewards, and consequences in place.

Until Sara and Annie were old enough to make or purchase their own lunches, they were allowed to buy them from the cafeteria once a week. On other days I made them. I was pretty easy with choices, but careful too. The girls gained weight easily, just as Ric and I did. They picked what they wanted among fairly healthy options: a sandwich, chips, and fruit were the norm. Occasionally I'd let them buy prepackaged Lunchables from the grocery store. I liked to get up early to have a little quiet time before the onslaught, and while putting their lunches together I often remembered my own school days when trading lunch items was a big deal.

Jenna arrived just before the new school year began. She was assigned the same third grade teacher Annie had, and I knew her well. The evening of Jenna's back-to-school night, I sat on my hands in the classroom. At forty-seven, I was the oldest parent by far. I had made school volunteering my life when the girls were there. I started by helping once a week in Sara's kindergarten class. By her fourth-grade year I was PTA president, and a year later I was elected to the Martinez school board. Enough. I was not going to volunteer again.

Chuck Benson had been the principal for all the years Sara and Annie were at John Swett. He was now an assistant superintendent at the school district office. In his place was Mike Jones, a friendly man whom I knew well. My second four-year term on the school board had ended the previous year, and I'd declined to run for reelection. Working at Olympic High School made it too difficult to do both jobs well.

In November, Mike called me at work. "Alice, we have a little problem with Jenna."

My stomach sank. "What's the matter?"

"She owes the cafeteria fifteen dollars, and I thought you should know about it."

"Oh, my God. What's that about? She takes her lunch almost every day. There's no need for her to borrow money for lunch."

"I had a feeling that was the case," said Mike. "What would you like me to do?"

My heart raced and I began to boil. Either she was throwing away the lunches I made for her, or, more likely, she ate the lunch at snack time and told the cafeteria lady I forgot to give her money. She was already overweight, and being diligent about what she ate was important to me. I wanted to throttle her. "Mike, you don't need to do anything other than tell the cafeteria to never lend Jenna any money."

"No problem," said Mike. "Good luck." Mike and most of the other teachers knew about Jenna's background. I had a solid support system at school.

I was glad I had time to think about what I would say to Jenna before I picked her up from the after-school program. I signed her out and

led the way back to the car. She got in, silent.
Most days I tried to make small talk with her,
but this time I was still seething. When we got
home and walked into the house, I told her to
put her backpack in her room and meet me in
the living room.

We sat on the couch. "Mr. Jones called me at
work today." Silence. "He told me you borrowed
lunch money many times." Nothing. "Why did
you do that?"

Jenna looked at me, her eyes blank, seeming to
look through me. I breathed in and out, counting
to ten.

"You have absolutely no reason to borrow
money. From now on, I'll make your lunch every
day. Mr. Jones told the cafeteria you may never
borrow money again." No response. "Now go to
your room."

She left, silent and obedient, showing no feeling. Why was Jenna like no other child I knew?
I sat there thinking about her tortured past. I
worked with teens at Olympic whose upbring-
ings were nearly as bad as hers, yet they showed
natural emotions: anger, laughter, love, sorrow.
Her behavior made no sense to me.

8

Junkyard

Even after we became Jenna's guardians, Ric's dad continued to enable Crystal. One example: Mom and Dad had but one car at a time throughout their long marriage. Before he retired, Dad carpooled with three men who also worked at the Shell Oil Refinery. Three weeks a month, Mom had the car, and during the one week when he drove it she went without. They had bought their first super-sized wagon in the mid-1960s and were on their third when Jenna moved in with us. Dad decided, finally, they no longer needed a big car and bought a used Toyota Camry. He gave the old Chevy wagon to Crystal.

Soon after, he received a ticket for his car

being parked in one spot for more than seventy-two hours. He hadn't done the paperwork to change ownership, so the authorities notified him rather than Crystal. He got another ticket. We guessed she was living in the car. A third notice followed stating the car had been towed to a scrapyard.

Jenna overheard Dad telling us about the car's fate. The next day she told me, "I need to get something from the station wagon."

I responded, "No, you don't. I'm sure all that was in the car was junk. I don't think it's a sight you want to see." She clammed up.

Within an hour, Dad was at our door; Jenna had called him and convinced him to take her to the car. I was upset about his decision, but I didn't want to argue. I went along with them.

When we reached the yard, an employee directed us to the wagon. We passed wrecked cars, burned-out cars, stripped-down cars. We walked down a slope and found the Green Machine, as Ric's younger brothers called it. I stopped. It was filled to the brim with crap. Except for a small space by the steering wheel, it was clogged with food wrappers, dirty clothes, blankets, boxes, and God knew what else. It reeked of rotting garbage. Jenna was determined to search for what she wanted, but she wouldn't (I expected couldn't) tell us what it was. I opened the rear door. The seats were folded down flat, and the entire space was full. I half expected to find bloodied tampons in the mix.

I walked away. Jenna kept looking, finally extracting a filthy stuffed blue bunny. I was certain she'd never seen it before because her mother was evicted more often than she stayed in one place, but I let her take it.

Jenna tried her hardest to latch onto anything remotely connected to her mother, wanting a love that didn't exist. It broke my heart. What would that woman do next?

9

Lost

After the two college summers Ric and I worked in the Sierraville area north of Truckee, I was determined to live full time in the mountains at some point. For years I drove around in my Miata, its license plate framed with my mantra: "All I want is a cabin in the woods." After much dreaming, discussing, and disagreeing, in 1999 Ric and I chose Boonville for our retirement, a tiny town in Mendocino County. It was in the middle of the Anderson Valley, twenty-five miles from the Pacific Ocean. In the early days, hops, sheep, and apples fueled the main economy. Logging followed; at one time there were forty redwood mills in the valley. That industry died out in the 1970s. Most orchards and open land slowly converted to fields of wine grapes. By the late 1990s, there were forty wineries in the valley. Marijuana, grown illegally, was an unspoken but major crop.

Three friends of ours had relocated to Anderson Valley, an added bonus. Barbara and I had worked together at Olympic High School, and she moved into her grandparents' vacant house when she retired. Wally and Sue had moved from the Bay Area. We visited them some years before when we were considering ideas for our future home. We drove down their long, wooded driveway to find their beautiful log home nestled under huge oak and madrone trees.

Ric turned to me, laughed and said, "Is this a setup?"

In 1999 Jenna remained an unhappy, sullen child. She did poorly in class. The after-school staff assured me she was no problem there, but with us she seemed empty. Certainly she was depressed. Our efforts to make her feel a part of our family were entirely one sided.

Ric didn't plan to retire for anther ten years, but I was anxious. I began looking for property in the summer while he was working 24/7 due to a huge project at the refinery. I found a friendly local realtor, and in October he showed us an undeveloped sixteen-acre parcel near Boonville. It was heavily wooded, and most of it was extremely steep. From a relatively flat ridgetop, it descended to seasonal Honey Creek and then part way up the other side. It was remote, yet we had nearby neighbors, and town was a ten-minute drive away. Once we removed some trees, the view from an excellent house site would be of undeveloped ridges to the south. In my mind it was perfect. Only stars would light up the nighttime sky.

Ric hesitated. "I thought we might live across the valley, where there are open areas and oak woodlands."

I elbowed him. "What is it about a cabin in the woods that you do not understand? Besides, I looked at properties across the valley, and any open land is exorbitant because of the potential for vineyards."

It took him a week to make up his mind, but in November the sale was in escrow, due to become ours in early January.

On a Saturday, with nine-year-old Jenna in the back seat, we drove up to Boonville from Martinez to meet with our realtor, Doug Johnson. We rode three miles from town in his battered Isuzu and then turned onto a steep gravel road. The closer we got to the top, the darker the dense woods became. As we entered our property, limbs from an overgrown logging road scratched his car. I should have realized Jenna would be spooked by the drive, but I was too excited to think about her needs.

Ric wanted to hike the entire boundary of our property to make sure there were no surprises. The first time we had visited, I'd joined Ric and Doug as we slipped and slid down the steep wooded hillside to the creek below and clawed our way back, pulling ourselves up by roots and trunks. There were no trails. This time I decided to hang out with Jenna and wait for them to finish their exploration.

The land had been logged in the 1960s. Since then, leftover coast redwoods had grown larger, and other species filled in the open spaces. First grew manzanita shrubs, then Douglas fir, madrone, and tanoak. The house site was a gentle slope where fir trees had shaded a stand of manzanita. The shrubs had all died, leaving blackened skeletons, nature's art.

After Ric and Doug disappeared, I sat down. I grabbed a stick and began poking it in the duff. Jenna stood above me.

"What are you doing?" she asked.

"I'm sitting in the dirt."

"But you'll get dirty."

"I like dirt."

"Aren't you afraid?"

"Afraid of what?"

"Afraid you'll get lost."

I looked up at her. She stood stiff, eyes wide. "No, I know exactly where I am. The car is right down there. See it? We drove up from town, and I know how to get back. Uncle Ric and Doug will return shortly, and then we'll go home." I patted the ground. "Sit with me."

She sat, disliking the choice, still taut with unease.

For my part, I was filled with joy, thinking this forest was nearly mine. Not a campground or a public forest. Mine. I whacked the trunk of a small madrone with the stick. My very own woods.

"Now what are you doing?" Jenna's fear interrupted my reverie.

"Enjoying the moment." I looked at her. "This is a special time for me." My heart was calm, serene. I listened to bugs clicking in the trees while this child, abandoned by the world, hunched her shoulders and stared at her feet.

10

A Different Side of Me

In fall 1999 my life was ramping up, but Jenna wasn't happy. We settled into taking care of her needs and parenting her as best we could. Her issues were sad and heartbreaking. She didn't return our hugs, she ignored our words of love, and she kept her emotions locked up most of the time—but we coped.

I was excited that my teaching career was over. The year in a classroom had been difficult for me, and I longed to get back to the College/Career Center. But I didn't exactly get my wish. Although Marcie had found another teacher to take my place, she asked if I would take on a temporary role for the new school year. The woman who took my place as College/Career Advisor would stay in the interim. My job now was threefold: I taught Transitions, the job skills class I enjoyed; I managed the biweekly orientations for new students; and I was now the coordinator of our school's accreditation process.

Accreditation was complicated. Throughout the fall, teams of teachers analyzed how well students were learning and the school was functioning. Each team was to write up its findings, and together the staff would discuss what we would do to improve student learning. All would be combined in a large report. My job was to nudge the teachers to do what was required of them and to put everyone's submissions together in a coherent way. A team of teachers and administrators from other alternative schools would read the report, visit our school in the spring, and give us their findings. A good review would mean an accreditation of up to six years; a poor one would mean we would have to do the process all over again and implement improvement strategies right away. We were motivated to prove we were an excellent school.

When I started my job at Olympic in 1995, it took me no time to realize that the teachers there were as alternative as our students. They liked doing their own thing. The challenge of herding these cats in order to do the work necessary to complete the task was one I liked.

By October I found myself enthusiastic about all my new challenges. I was filled with energy. I no longer needed the sleep I had craved the year before. Now, six hours was more than enough. I juggled several balls easily, both at work and at home.

Ric noticed the change and was worried about me. Each of my older brothers had developed hypermania in their mid-forties, and he saw similarities in my behavior. Although I liked the new me and was certain there was nothing wrong with me, at Ric's request I went to see our family doctor and told him what was going on.

He said, "Your symptoms sound a little like bipolar syndrome, but perhaps you'll be like your brothers and stay on the happy side without experiencing the low, depressive end."

I decided he meant I was fine and carried on. I found my new personality to be great fun, but my family will tell you I became nearly impossible to live with. I knew everything, could accomplish anything, and was dismissively obnoxious. I talked over people and didn't listen to them. I cut people off. There was one important person in every conversation: me.

At one point Ric said to me, "You keep going on like this and you'll have nobody."

My response: "I don't care."

I was particularly boisterous in a staff meeting one day when my friend Jim passed me a note. "You might want to read this," he said. "It helped Gretchen and me understand our son." He had underlined *An Unquiet Mind* by Kay Jamison. I trusted him and decided to read the book, a bestseller in which the author describes her experiences with both manic and depressive episodes. I began to think Ric might be right.

The manic episode ran its course without lasting damage. Wikipedia says symptoms of mania often include "extravagant shopping, sexual adventures, or improbable commercial schemes." Fortunately, the worst thing I did was buy a stand-up bass so I could play with a group of teachers at school. We had developed a musical program to go along with a Civil War skit, and I played the washboard. In my heightened state, I thought playing the bass would be easy and fun. So I bought one for $750. I had never played a stringed instrument in my life. What was I thinking? I wasn't. Later I donated the bass to the school.

Gradually my mania disappeared, and I looked back at how truly obnoxious I had been. I'd loved it, but no one around me did. I decided to hope for the best; perhaps this was a one-time thing.

Throughout all this, I have no recollection of how Jenna responded to the different me.

Most likely I was oblivious to her needs, another symptom of mania.

11

Tragedy

In December, a year after we became Jenna's guardians, heartbreak struck our family. Annie was a freshman at Diablo Valley College (DVC) in nearby Pleasant Hill. She worked part time in the college's child development center and earned extra money by transporting a minivan full of boys to their homes after school in Concord. Ever the pied piper with kids, she was hired by the mother of two boys in Concord who had attended a summer day camp where Annie had been a counselor. Once other parents learned how responsible she was, she soon had a carful. Annie took care of eight-year-old Matt until the boys' mom returned from work. Michael, eleven, spent most of each afternoon playing with other kids outside their apartment building.

One day Michael wasn't waiting outside the middle school. The other boys told Annie he hadn't come to school. At the elementary school Matt told her his brother had stayed home sick. When Annie and Matt walked into their apartment, the TV was on but Michael wasn't in the living room. She walked down a corridor to the boys' bedroom—and was horrified: Michael hung from a belt on the post of his bunk bed. She yelled at Matt to call 911 and struggled to free Michael from the belt. Inside she knew he was long dead, but her CPR training kicked in and she tried to revive him, pumping his chest and blowing into his mouth continuously until paramedics arrived. They told her to sit on the couch with Matt.

The phone rang on my desk at Olympic. Without giving specifics except to say Annie was okay, a woman told me to come to the apartment. The fifteen-minute drive across town seemed endless. What could have happened? What was wrong with Annie? My mind swirled with possibilities. The social worker who had called me met me in the parking lot and told me there had been an accident. As she led me upstairs, I heard a woman keening in a downstairs apartment. My heart pounded.

I found Annie on the couch with her sweat-shirt hood pulled over her head, staring at the floor. She would neither look at me nor speak. My stomach cramped and I felt nauseous. Neurons exploded in my brain. I led Annie downstairs and put her in our minivan. Standing behind the car, the social worker told me what had happened and encouraged me to make an appointment at the Crisis Center as soon as I could. I hugged my listless daughter and held her leg as I drove home. She sat frozen, head bent within the hood of her sweatshirt.

I put Annie to bed. She lay on her back, immobile. She wouldn't speak. She remained limp. I called the Crisis Center in Walnut Creek. They had a seven o'clock opening. I called Ric at work, and until he got home I lay next to Annie, unable to find comforting words. She stared at the ceiling, seemingly comatose. I felt helpless, terrified, and numb. There was no way I could imagine what was going on inside her head.

I stayed with her until it was time to go. As I drove to the Crisis Center, I remembered that an acquaintance was its director. He and his wife had lost both their sons, one to suicide at twenty and the other to a car crash just a year later. Switching careers had helped him deal with his grief.

The center proved to be a life saver. Annie spent a year attending sessions regularly, first

being counseled and then supporting other griev-
ing teens. Counselors recommended she maintain
a close relationship with Matt, as the two of them
had a bond no one else could ever understand.
She made a shrine for Michael in her room, and
she often visited his gravesite.

Counselors at the center also helped me. They
told me to be there for Annie but not push her.
It took her more than two weeks to open up. The
details she told me—Michael's stiff body and his
swollen blue tongue, Matt's frozen state on the
couch when the paramedics arrived—were horrid
to listen to.

Michael had been a happy, popular kid.
His death was incomprehensible. For a while
we thought it had been a horrible accident, but
then we learned he had cleaned out his locker
and neatly piled his books in a classroom. There
was talk of problems with a girl, but there were
no notes, no clues.

At home, Jenna dragged me down. I often
found her staring at us in Annie's bedroom.
During the memorial service she was mute. She
seemed to be in the background all the time, silent
but watching. I never thought she might copy the
suicide; she was too passive. The act would take
a concerted effort—not at all her nature. Her
inability to express herself was understandable,

but I couldn't give her the attention and time she needed. Annie's needs were much more important to me.

I learned a critical thing about suicide: everyone thinks they are responsible. In early January, Annie ran into the house, yelling "Mom, Mom!" She grabbed me and looked beseechingly into my face. "It was my fault, Mom. I let the boys listen to rap music in the car, and I just heard one of the songs. It talks about hanging from a belt from a bunk bed." There was no consoling her.

She began to doubt herself: "I can never be a teacher after what I did to Michael. I didn't know. I didn't have any idea."

Fortunately, she stayed in school. Her professors allowed her to postpone her finals, and her supervisor at the child development center held her job until she returned.

Helping Annie deal with her grief was my focus. Gradually she became more of herself and was able to enroll for the spring semester at DVC. Working with children at the child development center there helped her move forward. Meanwhile, Jenna remained the same. Her presence felt like a deflated balloon releasing the last of its air. Despite a number of people who continually tried to boost her up—her therapist and school counselor, family members, friends—she made no movement toward thinking positively about herself. It was so hard to give her what I could when she didn't respond at all.

12

Mediation

Another year passed. Jenna was ten, and her behavior had not changed. She kept us at a distance, never allowing herself to feel comfortable in our home or to love us. She showed little emotion, neither anger nor happiness. We did all we could to make her feel like our daughter and part of our family, but our efforts failed. When she walked into a room, it seemed like she sucked the life right out of it. It was frustrating for all of us.

In 2000 Annie and Sara were in college; Annie was a sophomore at DVC and living at home, and Sara was a senior at San Francisco State University. They both felt the amount of time and energy Ric and I put into raising Jenna was excessive. When they were growing up, Ric's career had been so stressful and absorbing that he was rarely home. Shortly after Jenna came to live with us, a new position at the refinery allowed him to work forty hours a week, and he had much more time for Jenna. The girls resented the extra time he had for her, and I didn't blame them. Regardless, Jenna was ours and we were determined to do our best.

The abuse Jenna had suffered was extreme. All the counselors she had—Grace, those from school, and later, Linda, another private counselor—said the same thing: she was one of the most damaged children they had worked with. Some stories she told me privately were so awful they were plausible: Alan, Brandon's father, threw knives at the kids and their mother to terrify them; he beat Jenna with a metal chain and then made her wear turtleneck shirts to kindergarten to cover up the wounds.

She didn't tell us a lot about her past, but when she did—those stories aside—much of it seemed unbelievable. A common trait of hers was to try to best what someone casually said. For example, if I accidentally tripped over a crack in the sidewalk that day and said, "I'm sure glad I didn't break my ankle like my friend Janet did by stepping on a pine cone," Jenna would create her own story:

"My friend's mom broke her ankle on a sidewalk last week. They were shopping downtown and her mom tripped on a big crack. They had to call an ambulance and everything."

If Ric recalled playing chess with his grandpa, Jenna loved playing chess with Grandpa Carl. When Annie talked about a difficult test at school, Jenna's was harder. The details she invented within seconds were remarkable. She could make up a story on the spot faster that I thought possible, an incredibly exasperating talent. She lied more often than she told the truth. It did no good to contradict her or question her. She would either stare at us with empty eyes or say, "You don't have to believe me if you don't want to." All the lies she casually told us made the few serious things she said about her past more doubtful.

Having quality, peaceful family time at the dinner table was nearly impossible. If Annie talked about her day's events at college and she happened to look at Ric, Jenna would turn to me and start talking about something else: anything to break up the conversation. When we reminded Jenna to be a good listener, she either got angry or shut down.

We routinely checked to make sure she completed her homework, but it rarely arrived in class. Her teacher tried hard to come up with ways to encourage Jenna—such as matching her with a younger child for some fun reading time if she completed all her work for a week—but after two or three times, she reverted. Nothing captured her interest.

Every other week Jenna eagerly awaited a supervised visit with Crystal at the Social Services office. Too often her mother didn't show up, and it broke my heart to see Jenna's sad face. She pretended it didn't matter: another way to shove her feelings deep inside her.

A teacher at John Swett gave me some invaluable advice when I needed it most. She had recently adopted a four-year-old boy who had been severely abused, and her relationship with him was as challenging as ours was with Jenna. She recommended a book for me to read, *A Child Called "It"* by Dave Pelzer. When, as a teen, he finally spoke the truth in court about the horrors he endured at home, professionals found him to be one of the most abused children in the history of California. Even so, and even after being placed with caring foster parents for years, he always wanted to be with his mother, the same person who gave his three brothers love but locked him in a dark basement and made him drink bleach when he misbehaved. The book helped me put Jenna's feelings in perspective; I stopped expecting her to give up on her mom and love us instead.

For two years Ric and I went to the juvenile justice commission more times than we could count, taking hours off work only to find, time after time, that Crystal was given yet another chance. President Clinton's Welfare-to-Work reforms, which provided job training and placement in addition to time limits of assistance, had little impact in her case. She failed to comply with requirements—did not keep jobs assigned to her, check in with the social worker, or visit her children regularly. The county gave her chance after chance to prove herself capable of caring for herself and her children, and added six months to the federal time limit of eighteen months, much to our frustration. After two years she was finally forced to give up her parental rights to all three kids. We wanted to adopt Jenna, but she refused: Jenna might never give up the hope of returning to her mother. We became her legal guardians instead.

Ric and I were joyous when we ended our association with county Social Services as foster parents. All the meetings, hearings, phone calls, letters, and uncertainty ceased. We were free from the inefficient, bloated government bureaucracy. Before we met with the juvenile judge for the last time, Crystal, Ric, and I were required to agree on the type of visitation Crystal would be allowed to have with Jenna. The county arranged for the three of us to meet with a professional mediator at Contra Costa Juvenile Hall.

I sat in the hard chair next to Ric, waiting. We had no idea what this session would involve, but I was very glad we wouldn't have to meet with Crystal alone. Having a mediator present was reassuring.

"Are you nervous?" I asked Ric.

"A little, but mostly I'm irritated. One more meeting, taking time off from work, rushing, and then waiting. I've been thinking about the hearing when we were the last to be called after nearly two hours. Remember?"

I laughed. "How could I forget?"

We had been surrounded by filthy men in torn T-shirts, bruised women who looked like they hadn't slept in days, crying babies, and confused grandparents. Every time the bailiff appeared, he yelled a name and escorted people into the courtroom. A man and woman were brought in from opposite sides of the waiting room. They wore orange suits and shackles. After they were called, there was no one left but us. Thirty minutes later, the bailiff came out and shouted "Bonner" to the empty room.

I shook my head, remembering.

On this day, two women entered the conference room and introduced themselves. One was the mediator; the other was there to record the outcome of our session. We waited. Crystal was invariably late or missed required hearings altogether.

The door crashed open. "Sorry." Crystal pushed past the mediator and slumped into a corner chair. Her hair was greasy. She wore purple sunglasses. She reeked of unwashed body odor.

The mediator looked through a file in front of her, then spoke. "We're here today to reach agreement on a schedule of visitation for Crystal Ehrlich to see her daughter, Jenna."

Silence. *What next?* I wondered. A minute went by. "So what do we do?" I asked.

The mediator said, "I'm here to help you resolve any differences you might have. You all are to decide for yourselves. I'll step in if I'm needed." More silence. Crystal sat in the corner, chewing gum.

"Do you mind if we go into the hall?" I asked. Ric and I excused ourselves and stepped outside.

"I sure didn't expect this, did you? What should we do?" I asked.

"Well, if it was up to me, Crystal would never get to see Jenna again, but that's probably not going to fly."

I thought for a moment. "What about this? She can see her in a public place for an hour once every two weeks."

"That seems more than fair."

We went back into the conference room and sat down. We proposed our idea. Crystal said nothing. The mediator asked her if the schedule was acceptable.

"Whatever they want is fine with me." It was hard to know if she was high or truly didn't care. I am normally a caring, compassionate person, but in Crystal's case? Absolutely not. I had disliked her from the first time I met her. She had taken advantage of Ric's parents and treated them cruelly. She had abused her children, expected handouts from the government, and had little contact with Jenna even though she was free to call. In my mind she was scheming and mean—in a word, evil. I could not forgive her for wrecking the lives of her children.

Damn, I thought. *Why didn't we start with an offer to never let her see Jenna?*

"Is everyone in agreement?" asked the mediator. "If so, I'll have my assistant draw up the papers. You three will sign them. The last step will be to meet with the juvenile court judge in a few weeks to finalize the visitation arrangement."

The three left the room. "Was that weird, or what?" I asked.

"Par for the course, I'd say," said Ric. "One more wasted half day away from work and another court date to look forward to."

A month later we were in the courtroom of

Superior Court Judge Lois Haight. She specialized in juvenile cases. Known for her fierce independence and fairness, she was all about the best interests of children. Waiting at the back of the courtroom, we watched as other cases were heard. Jenna's social worker was near the front with her bulging cart full of files; that kind woman was incredibly overloaded with cases. We guessed two men and a woman dressed in suits were attorneys. There was no sign of Crystal.

When Jenna's case was called, Judge Haight took a few minutes to look over the papers in front of her. "Is the mother here?" she asked. Looking up, then shaking her head, she asked if we were present. We raised our hands. My hands were clammy. My body was rigid. I had no reason to be nervous, but the large, formal courtroom was intimidating and Jenna's future was at a crossroad.

"It appears the court has given the mother more than enough resources and time to regain custody of Jenna. I see that you and the mother have reached an agreement on visitation." We nodded. She raised her hand and pointed her finger, waggling it at us as she spoke. My heart pounded. She wasn't a person you wanted to disobey or argue with. "I want you to know you have full responsibility for this child. If you ever feel Jenna is in any danger around her mother, I want you to get her out of there right away. I am going to add that the mother must call twenty-four hours ahead to confirm each visit. Good luck. Next case."

As we walked out of the courtroom, Crystal slid around the corner of the hallway. She was wearing her purple sunglasses and her hair was stringy. A grungy guy in baggy pants followed. "We got held up in traffic," she said. "The off-ramp was all backed up."

Likely story, I thought.

"The hearing is over," said Ric. "You can see Jenna once every two weeks for an hour, but you have to call us twenty-four hours before to confirm the visit. Otherwise you'll have to reschedule. We'll agree on a place and time." We continued down the hallway and out of the courthouse into sunshine. I was so relieved I could hardly stand it.

"Let's go to Shorty's Bar," I said to Ric. "I need a stiff one."

Ric laughed. "Yes, ma'am. Right this way." He held out his arm and I put mine in his.

13

Canary in My Mind

Whistling is part of my soul. I'm spot-on with pitch, and harmonizing comes naturally. I particularly enjoy whistling to music on the radio. I have absolutely no talent for deciphering or memorizing words to songs. Tunes are what fuel me. Whistling is a subconscious part of my being.

In junior high school I became captivated by the whistle of my best friend's mother. Mrs. Smith warbled. She produced unique music as she worked on crossword puzzles while sitting in her antique writing chair in a corner of the living room. She warbled while she cooked and as she walked through the house. She used her tongue as she whistled to produce her tunes, but

I preferred a purer sound made directly through my lips. I vowed then to perfect my personal musical instrument.

I love music. I played saxophone in elementary school and took piano lessons. I sang in the school chorus and enjoyed singing church hymns with my mom. Alto harmony was our gift. It was inspiring to hear the deep reverberations resonating from the pipe organ in the nave of the Presbyterian church as we sang.

The more I whistled, the better at it I got. People began to comment about how beautiful it sounded, all the encouragement I needed to pursue my hobby.

In fall 2000, a year after my manic episode, I lost my instrument. Not on purpose—it just disappeared. I might as well have disappeared with it. At first my usual energy waned. I didn't feel like talking to people and had a hard time concentrating. It was hard to be productive. I didn't want to return to the Kaiser mental health clinic because the psychiatrist I had seen to treat my anxiety made me uncomfortable. He wore shiny, baggy slacks and rumpled shirts. His hair was greasy and long. He leaned back in his chair and peered at me over his glasses. He didn't seem interested in me other than to prescribe drugs. My therapist, Joyce, who helped diagnose my anxiety, would have been a good person to talk to, but I didn't have the energy to see her. I just wanted the feelings to go away. Within two years I had suffered from Graves' disease, was diagnosed with anxiety, became manic, and now was depressed, and all of it happened after Jenna entered my life.

For her part, Jenna, now in fifth grade, was still doing poorly in every way. She was an enormous strain on our family, especially me. Her therapy sessions with Grace McMahon were going nowhere. I met with her teacher often, but nothing she tried motivated Jenna. At home she was sullen and withdrawn. Trying to encourage her was exhausting.

The week before Christmas that year, I was a wreck. School vacation started late. My to-do list was endless. The house was a mess. My parents, aunt, and sister were to arrive December 21 from Southern California. Perfect setup for what was to come.

On the day my family was to arrive, I awoke feeling like I was spinning in a vortex. I couldn't get out of bed. A mountain of black weight held me to the mattress. Jenna was with her grandfather for the day, Ric was at work, and neither Annie nor Sara was home. It was 11:00 a.m. before my bladder forced me to make my way to the bathroom. As I lay in bed, I felt worthless and hopeless. Thoughts of suicide began to weave their way through my helplessness—I felt nothing else would relieve my pain. The easiest implement I could think of to kill myself was Ric's sharp fishing knife in our closet, but I didn't have the energy to get up and get it.

I heard car doors shutting and happy voices coming from our driveway mid-afternoon. I managed to go downstairs from our loft bedroom and meet my parents at the door.

"I'm sorry," I told them. "I'm feeling really depressed and I need to go back to bed. Ric will be home in a while."

Mom, Dad, my aunt, and my sister looked at me wide-eyed, their arms bursting with wrapped gifts and cans of cookies. After a moment they stepped inside.

"Sure, of course," Dad said. "We'll be fine. What can we do to help you?"

"Nothing," I said. "I just need to rest." I climbed back up the stairs and crawled under the covers.

They had never seen me in anything but a take-charge, all-together state. The previous Christmas in my manic state, I was thrilled to show them the stand-up bass I planned to play. Today they sat in the living room below me, worried and wondering what to do. After trying to talk to me and getting little response, Dad called Ric at work.

Ric came home and called Kaiser. An emergency therapist asked me over the phone if I had thoughts of hurting myself. I told her I did and, embarrassed that Ric was by my side, admitted his knife was my chosen method. He took me straightaway to the mental health clinic.

The car ride was a dull blur, but I remember sitting in the therapist's office with my head hanging between my knees, feeling heavy and lethargic. The therapist stressed the seriousness of my state of mind. She asked me if I would promise not to hurt myself, and I agreed. She told Ric he was to be in charge of me and to make sure someone was with me at all times.

My psychiatrist called the following day and suggested I try Depakote, a drug that might help in combination with the Paxil I already took for anxiety. Unfortunately, it would take four to six weeks before beginning to have a significant effect. The days dragged. I felt remote. I listened to family members converse throughout the holidays, but I had nothing to say. I followed Ric around like a puppy dog, doing whatever he told me to do.

One evening my family, including my brother and his wife and daughters, had tickets to attend a holiday version of the hilarious *Beach Blanket Babylon* in San Francisco. There was no way I could leave the house, so Annie volunteered to stay with me. She watched TV while I sat in front of it. Later, my brother told me Jenna dwelled on my illness that evening and wanted to talk about it with everyone. She didn't act concerned about me, he said. Rather, it was like she was boasting.

Before my parents returned to their home in Santa Barbara, Ric surprised me with an overnight holiday getaway he had planned for weeks. He knew I loved surprises, but it was rare that he could pull one off. I didn't want to disappoint him, so I agreed to go. As he drove through the Berkeley hills without telling me our destination, I felt a kind of terror I'd never experienced. It made no sense, but I dreaded whatever lay ahead. What I really wanted to do was crawl in the trunk of the car and huddle in a fetal ball. I ached, knowing I had ruined his thoughtful gesture. He held his hand on my thigh the entire drive except when he had to shift my Miata's gears. I was silent.

As we headed down toward the university, I thought we might be staying at the historic Claremont Hotel. My heart pounded. I breathed out as we passed the hotel's white towers that nestled in the hills above the city. As we approached the Bay Bridge a few minutes later, I guessed San Francisco was our destination.

Sure enough, as we parked the car Ric said, "Here we are." He had outdone himself. The doorman of the St. Francis Hotel opened my door as a valet took the keys from Ric. After registering, we walked up a grand staircase and rode an ancient elevator. Our room was small and dated, but oh-so special. Tears filled my eyes.

"I'm so sorry I ruined this wonderful surprise. I'm such a mess."

He smiled. "I wish I could have planned this for a better time, but let's try to make the most of it. Maybe being away from the stress of home will make you feel a little better."

Walking the streets of the city eased my load a little. Ric had reserved a dinner table at the Farallon, a unique restaurant on Union Square. I couldn't help but feel lighter when we were seated in the Pool Room, the arched ceiling of which had graced the Elks Club pool in the 1920s. Giant sea urchin chandeliers hung over our heads. The service and food were outstanding. I was glad we had come and promised Ric we'd do it again when I overcame my pathetic state.

Back home, however, I felt no better. Shortly before school vacation ended, I called my principal and told her I couldn't come back. She implored me to return. As the coordinator of the College/Career Center, I had a great deal of flexibility and could arrange my schedule according to my needs. I reluctantly agreed. I cancelled the job skills class that was to begin. I remember sitting for many days at my desk, staring at the floor.

While waiting for the Depakote to take effect,

I slept a lot and played endless solitaire. Annie and I competed in a gin rummy marathon, playing to 1,000 points. Jenna largely kept out of my way, but I often found her staring at me. Thank goodness Ric and Annie took charge and Sara helped when she could. We had the kind of supportive family we wanted to share with Jenna if she would only let us.

Gradually my energy returned. I was more effective at work and began to resume my regular duties. I initiated conversations. I shopped and cooked meals at home. One day I noticed I was whistling along to the radio. My canary sang again.

14

Respite

Having Jenna live with us could have caused fissures in our own family life and marriage. Ric and I knew we needed occasional breaks with help from friends and family. It didn't happen often; it's not easy to spend time with someone who deflates most every conversation. Sara and Annie were good about staying home with her if we asked them to, but we tried to limit our requests. They were busy young women, had little patience with Jenna, and resented the stress she caused us. Twice we asked Ric's brother, John, to take her for a weekend at his family's home in Davis. His children, Olivia and Zach, were either side of her age. We thought having some cousin time would be a good thing, but after a day or two, they were ready to send her home.

Jenna had one friend whose family never gave up on her. She met Bridget Nelson in third grade. Bridget, an only child of older parents, was immature and didn't make friends easily. I figured the two misfits were attracted to one another. Ric and I had an easy relationship with Bridget's parents, Nancy and Doug. The girls spent time together and nights at each other's homes every few weeks. Even though Jenna's friend transferred to the local Catholic school after fourth grade, they remained close. When they were in fifth grade, a Saturday outing tested the relationship between Jenna and the Nelsons. It was a warm spring day, and I was delighted when Nancy called to invite Jenna to Santa Cruz: a free day for us and a fun experience for her. I gave her some spending money when they drove up, and said, "Have a great time."

Jenna was sunburned but happy when they dropped her off after the long day. In her hands was a striped blue bathing suit. "Where did you get that cute swimsuit?"

"It was so warm, we wanted to go swimming in the ocean," she said. "I didn't bring my suit, so we looked and found this one on a rack outside a store for only five dollars. It fits perfectly."

The price sounded remarkable, but I didn't think to question her.

Three weeks later the phone rang. "Hi, Alice, it's Nancy. Did Jenna tell you I loaned her money to buy a swimsuit when we went to Santa Cruz?"

My shoulders slumped. "All she told me was the suit cost five dollars. I assumed she paid for it with the money I gave her."

A brief silence followed. "No," said Nancy, "the suit cost fifty dollars."

"Oh, no, here we go again. Thanks so much for calling. I'll be sure to drop a check by your house. We'll see what Jenna has to say. I almost hate to imagine it. I can't tell you how much I appreciate your hanging in there with us, Nancy."

"It's okay. I know deep down there's a good person waiting to blossom. I'm glad Doug and I can be here for her. Bridget gets it too and really wants to stay friends with her."

When I confronted Jenna, she gave me one of her vacant stares. I sent her to her room and seethed inside. Why couldn't she act like a normal kid: look embarrassed at being caught or argue with me? Her silence was exasperating. Her father ignored her, her mother neglected and abused her, her grandparents indulged her, and we were trying to help her. At times like this I felt utterly helpless.

Two people loved Jenna unconditionally: her grandfathers. Ric's dad took care of her whenever we asked, even when Ric's mom was debilitated by Alzheimer's. Dad found an ideal situation when Jenna was nine: a family lovingly cared for Mom and five other Alzheimer's patients, and Dad lived in a small apartment behind the home. He and Jenna were very close, but we tried to limit their time together. When she was with him, there was absolutely no structure. He felt so sorry for her that he gave her whatever she wanted whenever she wanted it. Cake and ice cream for breakfast? Watch TV all night long? No problem. It drove us crazy, but every month or so we desperately needed time to stay home alone or escape to our Anderson Valley property for the weekend.

Jenna's maternal grandfather, Bob, lived in southern Oregon. He tried very hard to maintain relationships among her and her two half-siblings, all born to his daughter. He and his ex-wife had adopted Crystal as an infant. Their marriage dissolved, largely because of Crystal, and Bob raised her. She was an incorrigible child. Bob told me a doctor once suggested she had a disruption of the bridge between the left and right sides of her brain; one half of the brain might not know what the other half was doing.

I was curious about that, and he gave me an example: When Crystal was little she had great difficulty learning to tie her shoes. If the bridge, the corpus callosum, didn't work properly, she might understand what she needed to do but not be able to make her fingers respond. I looked up the syndrome and found that new research indicated a broken bridge wasn't likely the culprit. I thought she was one of those kids who were impossibly unruly and then grew up worse despite sound parenting. The damage she had caused three innocent children was unforgivable. I often had to bite my lip to fulfill my self-imposed promise to never say anything negative about Jenna's mother in front of her.

Crystal left home when she was sixteen. It was shortly afterward that she met Ric's brother, Mark, and told his parents she was homeless. After Mark, two more men impregnated her. Since none of her partners stuck around, she used her children to wheedle what she could from her father and father-in-law.

Bob did his best for Jenna and her siblings, his only grandchildren. Through friends he found a couple in Antioch who wanted to adopt her brother Brandon. After two years in foster care, her sister Leticia was adopted by a single mother in Vacaville. At Bob's initiative, we all got together for picnics and at Christmas. During summers and school vacations, Bob took Jenna for a week at a time. We generally met him along Interstate

5 halfway between Martinez and his home near Medford. He and his second wife lived on five wooded acres in a small, beautiful house. Jenna thrived while she was with him. A former high school teacher, Bob was a loving yet firm grandfather. We treasured the few breaks he gave us each year and wished he lived closer.

On one occasion, events leading up to Jenna's visit with Bob made me want to strangle her. Returning from a week at Elwell Lakes Lodge, our favorite spot in the northern Sierras, we were on our way to meet Bob in the town of Mt. Shasta. We had stayed at Elwell every summer since Annie was three. Its old housekeeping cabins were on the edge of a huge glacial basin filled with pine and fir forests, with some forty small lakes, views that went on forever, and stunning wildflowers. During sleepless nights at home I often imagined myself hiking to the top of Mt. Elwell, one step at a time along the trail, trying to still my brain. The peak offered a magnificent 360-degree view. A steep cliff on the back side loomed over three mountain jewels: Wades Lake, Jamison Lake, and Rock Lake. My kind of heaven.

I was surprised Jenna liked the cabins since she was not used to the outdoors. She didn't hike with us, but she made friends with kids in other cabins. She loved playing games in the rec hall during the day and flashlight tag at night. Her behavior, endearing herself to others instead of us, reminded me of our large family reunion in Bend, Oregon, the previous summer when she was ten. Rather than having fun with cousins her age, she immediately became "best friends" with a little girl whose family was in the condominium below ours. She chose strangers over our relatives.

We made a long northerly detour to meet Bob. Before we left Elwell, I asked Jenna to use the one phone at the resort to let him know we were on our way. We were crowded into our Ford pickup: Ric and his brother John were in the front and Jenna, our nephew Zach, and I sat in the narrow back seat. We planned to meet Bob at the visitor center in Mt. Shasta and then drive the four more hours home.

As we pulled into the center's parking lot, Jenna said, "I told Grandpa I'd call him when we got here."

I was livid. "What? It's a two-hour drive from his house to here. What were you thinking? You were supposed to tell him we were leaving and we'd be there in about three and a half hours."

"I did what I thought I was supposed to do." She stared out the window, and, in typical Jenna fashion, remained silent. I knew I had asked her to tell Bob our expected arrival time. Another lie and more passive-aggressive behavior.

Ric raised his voice. "I cannot believe you did that, Jenna."

We looked at each another. Why on earth did I let her make the arrangements instead of talking to Bob myself? Probably because I was so looking forward to our respite from Jenna, I wasn't thinking clearly. And my own kids would have done what I asked. How hard was it? Moments like this were exactly why we needed a break.

The day was warm, and the visitor center's lawns were inviting after we'd been crammed in the truck for hours. I called Bob. There was nothing to do but wait for him to arrive. As much as I wanted to yell at Jenna, I lay on the grass, trying to ease my ire by thinking of every step on the trail to the peak of Mt. Elwell. Ric paced the parking lot, John and Zach went in search of something to eat, and Jenna sat in the truck, acting oblivious to what she'd put us through.

Fortunately, throughout all of that, Ric and I had our own respite in Boonville. Ever since we purchased the property in 2000, if our girls or Ric's dad were able to look after Jenna, we made the two-and-a-half-hour trip about twice a month. Norma, a friend from work, sold us a twenty-foot travel trailer for $1,000. It wasn't worth more than that. Its roof leaked, so we built a structure over it to keep out the rain. It was fun to cut and peel small trees for rafters. Frosted corrugated plastic roofing allowed light to filter through. It also served as a shelter for an adjacent deck we constructed. When we lay in bed—I was next to the wall—I could see through to the ground where globs of caulking no longer sealed the cracks. Mice and chipmunks were a constant problem. When we left each Sunday, we made sure everything edible was sealed tightly in plastic or metal containers.

We named our place Bonner Ridge. A jumper cable hookup from our minivan's battery to the trailer's battery supplied electricity, and as long as we drove somewhere each day, we had power. Three times we forgot to do that and found the car battery dead. We met friendly neighbors each time by walking to their homes to ask for a jump-start.

Ric built a fireplace out of concrete blocks and set up an old Weber BBQ next to it. We dug a pit for an outhouse and named it Aunt Ellen after the one at Ric's grandparents' cottage in northern Wisconsin. With the four-burner cooktop, oven, small refrigerator, Aunt Ellen, the grill, and a fireplace, we had a perfect permanent campsite. We brought water from home in five-gallon jugs and took showers at our friend Barbara's home in nearby Philo. My favorite winter evening activity was the fulfillment of a dream I'd had since I was a little girl. Ric made a long-handled fork I used to toast cheese over an open fire, and I spread it on rustic bread for a special treat. It made me feel like the children's book character Heidi at her grandfather's hut in the Swiss Alps.

15

The Parent Project

I stood outside Jerry's office at Olympic High School, waiting for him to finish his phone call. I loved to chat with him when I had a few minutes. He was the psychologist for the Alliance Program, a small school located on the Olympic campus for high school students who had severe emotional and/or behavioral problems. Three years prior, the placement of the program at Olympic had been controversial. Several Olympic teachers didn't want Alliance students or their staff sharing our space. I welcomed them; I liked the teachers, aides, and counselors, and I felt there was a fine line between the issues of Olympic at-risk kids and those at Alliance. Two of their students successfully completed my job skills class that fall, a big accomplishment for them and a good indicator to me that the two schools were compatible.

"Alice," Jerry said, "have you ever met Manny, another high school psychologist in the district?"

"No, I haven't. Why?"

"We're going to offer an evening program here, and I think you might want to sign up. It's called the Parent Project, and it's for parents who have teenagers who are out of control."

I thought for a moment. Jenna was eleven, in the sixth grade. Her teenage years were just around the corner. It didn't take a crystal ball to predict sex, drugs, and rock and roll in her future. Well, maybe not the music. I signed up.

Three weeks later, I sat in my own Career Center as a student with fourteen other adults. Some were in pairs, others were single. Ric was home with Jenna. I looked around. As much as I didn't want to make judgments, I surmised the parents themselves might be cause for their kids' problems: ragged, dirty shirts on two of the men; gold lamé stretch pants, bleached hair, and high heels on one woman; a suspiciously druggie look to another, her hair stringy and her skin sallow. I felt decidedly out of place.

Jerry spoke first. "Hi, everyone. We're going to be together for the next eight weeks, every

Wednesday evening. We hope you will complete the class, not only to learn some useful tools but also to build close relationships in order to continue to support one another." He continued. "I asked each one of you to bring a baby picture of your son or daughter. If you forgot, close your eyes and picture him or her as a baby."

Not only did I not have a photo, but I could hardly picture Jenna as a baby. We had spent very little time with her then. Being around her with her dad, Mark, and her mom, Crystal, made us sick with worry about her future.

I closed my eyes, pretending to see a photo of a cute, brown-haired little girl with Mark's wide smile. Jerry interrupted my reverie. "That sweet baby you see is the same person who causes you such grief today." He paused. "The first assignment is for you to tell your son or daughter out loud every day that you love him or her. Do you think you can do that?"

I knew I could, but I doubted it would have much of an effect. Nothing else I had tried for the past three years had worked. Other parents nodded their heads, and I imagined their thoughts were the same as mine. I looked around again and reprimanded myself for making hasty first impressions.

Manny got up next and handed us thin packets. "This is a questionnaire for you to fill out right now. We want to get to know your teen better. Please work independently. When you complete the survey, pass it back to me. I'll send them in for analysis, and I'll give you the results next week."

I picked up a pencil and read the first question: "What does your child do when he or she has time to him or herself?" Unless I allowed her to watch TV or planned something for her to do, Jenna sat and did nothing. She didn't read, play outside, work on crafts, or draw. She was happy to interact with other people, but by herself? She sat. Other questions were similarly difficult to answer. I completed the survey as best I could and gave it back to Manny.

Our normal parenting style wasn't effective with Jenna. Ric and I had always successfully used consequences and rewards with Sara and Annie. Jenna cared about nothing, positive or negative. Material things meant nothing to her. She and her family were evicted frequently, and when they moved they took a few possessions with them in a plastic garbage bag and left the rest. If we gave her a consequence of no TV, she sat in her room or on the couch. If the reward for turning in her homework for a week was to have a friend stay over on the weekend, she might or might not do it. The loss of the reward was no big deal to her.

A week later and an hour before the Parent Project class, Manny and Jerry were in my room, moving tables and going over their notes. Manny walked to my desk.

"Alice, I want to talk to you about the results of the questionnaire."

"Okay, let me have it."

"I've never seen results that show such a depressed kid as Jenna's." I was surprised, but not overly so, given her tragic background.

"That's why I'm here. If you have any suggestions for how my husband and I might deal with her, I'd love to hear them. Like I told you before, we're getting nowhere with her. She's like an empty bag. A void seems to exist within her, like she has no soul." Manny looked at me with compassion, squeezed my shoulder, and went back to work setting up the room.

I learned a lot in the class. We were reminded that our children lived in a home that belonged to us, not them. One couple's seventeen-year-old son was hooked on methamphetamine; he came and went as he pleased, didn't go to school, was out all night. Manny and Jerry suggested they take the bedroom door off its hinges and tell their son (and mean it) they would call the police if he didn't obey their rules. They had to prepare themselves to draw a rigid line in the sand. At the minimum, drugs and truancy were punishable by law.

They stressed how important it was to remain calm with our teenager. I thought that might be difficult for many of the parents, given the argumentative interactions between them, but it would be easy for Ric and me. We rarely raised our voices in anger, and we had experience fielding arguments.

As inappropriate as it might have seemed to others, when I felt hopeless I compared Jenna to the guide dog puppy Annie raised when she was fourteen. Tarragon was a goofy, unruly puppy until she donned her official little green coat and went out in public; only then did she consistently respond to commands. From the get-go, our own dog, Curly, disliked her because she was always in his face, nudging and licking him. We had to be diligent for the sixteen months we had her, or normally friendly Curly would snap at her. I never had a dog as difficult to train as she, but knowing she wasn't truly ours made tolerating her much easier. It would also make it relatively easy to give her up. Jenna was a human, of course, not a dog. Still, the way things were going, I had little hope she would remain part of our family after she turned eighteen. We offered to adopt her from the beginning, but she refused in much the same way as she pushed away our love and caring. All of us wanted her to stay with us and become a happy, healthy person. I think because I wanted to protect myself, I began to see her as temporary, like Tarragon.

The most interesting lesson I took away from the Parent Project was TEASPOT: "Take everything away for a short period of time." We talked about brain development in adolescents. They live in the moment, so grounding them for a month is no different than for two days. They think, "Why bother to comply with rules at all?" Manny and Jerry had us make a list of everything important to our child: TV, music, fast food, headphones (few teens had cell phones then), having friends over, going to a movie. We then made a list of rules we could stick to. If one was broken, we would take away something from the list for a day. Depending on the severity of the infraction, we were to remove items until everything was taken away, but never for more than a week. Beyond that would be meaningless to the teen.

I liked the idea and eagerly began thinking of Jenna's likes. Then I stopped. I realized there was absolutely nothing Jenna coveted enough to get a reaction if I took it away. Our if/then parenting style had little effect on her, so why would this work? I left the program willing to give TEASPOT a try, and I enjoyed the class, but I wasn't hopeful it would be successful with Jenna.

As I guessed, TEASPOT had no effect on Jenna. Over time, the advice I received, "Give her a healthy home life," helped me. I lowered my expectations. If we couldn't fix her, we could at least surround her with safety, care, and love when she let us.

I got very tired of people telling me, "Alice, you're a saint." I certainly didn't feel like one. Occasionally I resented that few people other than Jenna's grandfathers and the Nelsons offered to help us out.

Ric and I often talked about the helplessness we felt.

"Sometimes I feel like taking care of Jenna is just a job," I told Ric one day.

He replied, "You might be on to something. It sounds callous, but since we get absolutely nothing from Jenna while we give her everything we can, maybe we should see this as a job. The idea makes me feel better. Resigned, but better."

"I think you're right. From now on I'll continue to have hope but consider this business rather than an emotional project. You know, it's really hard for me to spend all day with troubled kids at Olympic and then come home to Jenna. Especially since some of my students, as messed up as they are, still want to be somebody, someone different from their own parents. I'm not sure if I ever told you, but in my job skills class I start out with three questions: Who are you, what do you want, and how are you going to get there? Do you know what virtually all of them want?"

"I can't guess," said Ric.

"A family and a big house behind a white picket fence. Isn't that something? Why can't Jenna be like that?"

16

Jenna's Secret

After three lackluster years with Grace McMahon, I decided we needed to find a therapist who had more specific expectations of Jenna. Grace was very nice, but I felt Jenna often shined her on, just as she did us. Their relationship had become a bit tainted early on. I had encouraged Dad Bonner to meet with Grace. Afterward he proceeded to tell Crystal some of what they talked about. Crystal flipped out and directed her anger at Jenna the next time she saw her. I don't think Jenna trusted Grace after that.

I called Manny from the Parent Project. He recommended Linda Sanchez. It was hard for me to end the relationship with Grace, but once I did, I felt relief. We needed a fresh start. Manny told me Linda used a relatively new treatment called EMDR (Eye Movement Desensitization and Reprocessing), a type of hypnosis used to help people who have had serious trauma or who suffer from post-traumatic stress disorder. He thought the treatment might be successful with Jenna.

I talked with Linda on the phone, described Jenna's background, and made an appointment to bring Jenna to see her. Her small office was in a professional building next to the freeway south of Walnut Creek in Alamo: easy access as long as the late afternoon traffic wasn't too terrible. Linda ushered us in and welcomed us. She was in her early forties, an attractive woman with black hair and blue eyes.

Both Jenna and I liked her right away. She was direct yet friendly. She told Jenna that everything they talked about was confidential, but if what Jenna shared indicated she wanted to harm herself, Linda would tell me. Jenna agreed to meet with her. I waited in the car with a good book, time to myself I thoroughly enjoyed.

Linda and I communicated, but we never discussed specifics. After three months she felt Jenna was making progress, but she wanted my permission to try EMDR.

"I truly think it will help her get beyond some of the trauma she suffered," she said.

At the beginning of the next session, Linda asked me to join Jenna. She held up a black metal wand about eighteen inches long, studded with tiny lights. She turned it on, and the lights tripped back and forth. "I've talked about this process with Jenna and she's willing to give it a try, but I wanted to show it to you as well. As the lights flash, I will ask Jenna to focus on them and think about traumatic memories related to a specific event. We're not exactly sure how it works, but we think as the eyes track the lights, people can process disturbing feelings, transform their meanings, and shift to a firm belief that they survived the event and are strong. It's hard to explain, but it's often very effective."

I said, "Jenna, is this okay with you?"

"Linda and I have already talked about it, and I want to get started." I was surprised and happy Jenna seemed to be in charge of her treatment, letting me know that it was her, not me, who called the shots. That was encouraging.

Three weeks later Linda again asked me to join them at the beginning of the session.

"Jenna wants to talk to you about her experience with EMDR."

Jenna looked directly at me. "You know how terrible Alan was, and I've told you about some of the mean things he did to me and my family." I nodded. "What I didn't tell you was that he told me again and again he would kill me if I ever told anyone. I believed him and have been terrified. The EMDR was amazing. I now have no fear of him. He can never hurt me again."

"Wow," I said. "That's amazing. I'm so very proud of you, and I appreciate your sharing with me. That's fabulous, Jenna."

A weight seemed to lift off her as we left Linda's office. She was chatty—so unusual—and told me about the process. "It was really interesting. As the lights flashed I felt myself go into sort of a trance. Linda talked to me quietly. She first had me describe what Alan did to me and how he made me feel. Then she helped me understand I could let all my fear go and leave him behind. He's a terrible person. I wish he wasn't Brandon's father."

As we drove home, I was hopeful, again.

17

Sara's Wedding

The summer before Jenna's seventh-grade year, 2002, was extra stressful for me at home due to Sara's upcoming wedding in September. I truly didn't want to spend much time planning the event with her; formal weddings are not my cup of tea. I had planned my own, a simple celebration in 1974. We chose an outdoor setting in Plumas-Eureka State Park near where we had worked before Ric and I graduated from UC Davis. I embroidered wildflowers on my dress and wore daisies in my hair. Ric and I invited immediate family and friends who were close to both of us. Ric's family's minister came up from Concord to perform the short ceremony in a forest where log benches normally held campers for ranger talks. Afterward we all walked from the park up the road to Johnsville, an old mining town. Our reception was held in a gold mining–themed restaurant there, the Iron Door.

When Sara and Dave, her boyfriend of six years, announced their engagement, I told Sara we would give her a budget but the wedding was hers to plan. She could create the event she had dreamed about since she was little and I would be there if she needed me. She grabbed my arm and said, "I need you every step of the way." *Oh, boy,* I thought. *Here we go.*

She and Dave had met a month before she left for college. He grew up in Martinez not far from our home, but he went to Catholic schools and their paths had never crossed before. Ric and I didn't dislike him, but we also didn't think he was a good match for Sara. She was outgoing and set goals for herself. Extremely shy, he wasn't as ambitious as she was. It was three years before he would speak more than a few words to us. It didn't help that the first time I met him, he was in Sara's bed. I knocked on her bedroom door in our basement to give her a phone message, opened it a crack—Sara had leaped up to keep it closed—and saw a boy's back wrapped in the sheet.

Sara spent two years researching colleges all over the country and finally picked the University of Oregon, a fine school with costly out-of-state tuition. Having known Dave but a month before she left, once she arrived in Eugene she spent all her savings calling him long distance and secretly flying home twice to see him. She was beyond miserable. After fruitless cajoling on our part, she moved home before Christmas. Although she finished the quarter, none of her credits qualified for a transfer to a school based on semesters. We were not at all happy.

In January she joined Dave at Diablo Valley College. Two years later both transferred to San Francisco State and lived in a Daly City apartment. I tried to remain open-minded. Giving her my honest opinion of Dave would likely have backfired, so I held out hope she would eventually come to realize he wasn't for her. Meanwhile I consoled myself with two positives: he liked kids and dogs. While at DVC he worked at an after-school day care center and enjoyed playing with our beloved dog, Curly. When he and Sara came home from San Francisco to do laundry on weekends, he tutored Jenna in math. She resisted our help but felt special receiving the attention of her cousin's boyfriend.

The couple moved back to Martinez after they graduated and lived in a small house his parents had purchased as a rental. Sara—and I—began planning their wedding in the fall, a year before the event. The first thing I told her was, "I don't care where you have it, but I don't want the stress of having it at our house." They (Sara) decided they wanted to have both the ceremony and reception at the same venue, and together we found a beautiful spot in Walnut Creek. The U-shaped Quail Court Restaurant was situated around a Tuscan-style courtyard filled with tiny lights. Two sides were dining rooms; the third was a bar. Its dark blue ceiling twinkled with lighted stars while poetry stanzas flowed across the walls. Outside the restaurant, a stunning Benny Bufano sculpture, a stylized mother and children made of stone, stood at the end of a large lawn surrounded by giant oaks. A perfect wedding venue. It was a charming place and I loved the friendly owner's name, George Bernard Shaw.

Sara was enthralled with the details. We shopped at David's Bridal, where we found a perfect ivory, pastel-beaded dress and a coordinating gown for Olivia, our ten-year-old niece from Davis who was to be the flower girl. Annie, the maid of honor, Jenna, the junior bridesmaid, and two of Sara's good friends were fitted by a dressmaker in Pleasant Hill. Sara feared Jenna would put a damper on the happy festivities, but she knew including her was the right thing to do. Jenna was excited to be a part of it.

Through friends I found a cake maker and a

photographer. At Quail Court we sampled hors d'oeuvres for the reception with Dave and his parents. Sara ordered rose petals for the aisle, and we consulted two Martinez friends of mine for other decorations. Dave wasn't thrilled about picking registry items with Sara and me but did his best to please Sara.

I tried to be helpful and calm, but both Ric and I truly had our doubts about the pair. They did not seem to be well-suited lifetime partners. All we could do was hope for the best.

After graduation Dave had taken a job as a bank teller in San Rafael, a forty-five-minute commute. He wasn't sure what he wanted to do for the long term. Sara, a psychology major, became a teacher at a Gymboree play center and soon became manager. Corporate management appealed to her, and she saw future opportunities there. She hired Annie part time, and the two of them had fun working together with infants, toddlers, and their parents. Under Sara's leadership her site gained significant membership.

Trouble began to brew in the spring. Dave had a coworker, Hannah, who was engaged. The two couples double-dated a few times, but Sara told me she felt Hannah was more interested in Dave than in her own boyfriend. She had a bad feeling about her. Hannah often called Dave at home. Although Sara was concerned, Dave told her they were just friends. Later, the girls' cousin Becca told Annie she had seen Dave and a girl at a movie theater near where Becca lived in San Rafael.

The wedding plans proceeded. Friends gave them a couple's wedding shower and invitations were sent. I kept track of gifts that were delivered. Both Dave's family and ours were large. Some 100 people were coming from as far away as New York. We helped coordinate lodging for our out-of-town guests.

Three weeks before the wedding, we decided to take a short family trip, likely the last we'd ever have as a foursome. My work friend Jim owned a cabin at Lake Tahoe he occasionally rented, a perfect retreat for us. We did not invite Jenna. We knew it would hurt her feelings, but after four years of her pushing us away, we also knew that her way of dousing family fun would damper the weekend. She stayed with her Grandpa Carl. We had a blast looking at old slides and movies of the girls growing up, playing board games, and cooking together. As a surprise Ric and I brought our little wooden sushi maker. While I stirred sticky rice, Sara prepped and Ric and Annie wrapped folded napkins around their heads to emulate sushi chefs. On a brilliant blue Saturday, we rode the MS *Dixie* paddle wheeler across the lake's crystalline waters. We all agreed it was one of the best times we'd had together.

The couple got their marriage license Monday morning before the Sunday wedding. That day Ric flew to LA for a meeting. Tuesday Sara called me from Dave's parents' home.

She gulped and sobbed as she garbled, "Mom, Dave says he doesn't want to marry me."

My gut wrenched. "I'll be right over." Maria and Guido's house was ten minutes from ours. When I entered, I found all of them on a large couch: Dave curled up in a ball, Sara weeping, and the parents sitting silently, holding hands.

Maria said, "Dave says he doesn't love Sara and doesn't want to get married."

Dave said nothing.

My first thought: *What a weak dope. He waits until five days before the wedding to confess?* I was livid. I held Sara close. Dave rolled over and half sat up. He looked like a blubbering dolt with red eyes, drooping eyelids, and a raw face. *We've already paid for the venue, the food, the photographer, the dresses, everything but the cake. What an absolute asshole.*

After awkwardly and briefly talking to them, I took Sara home. "It's Hannah, isn't it," I said as we drove.

She nodded, wiped her face, and blew her

nose on a Kleenex. "How could I be such a fool? She kept calling and calling, no doubt insisting he break it off. He told me she was having difficulties and needed a friend. I wanted to believe him."

"You did what any person would do. I know you don't want to hear this, but it's so much better that you found out now rather than later. I just wish he'd have acted like a man."

"I can't believe it, Mom. What are we going to do? Everyone is coming!"

"Don't worry, taking care of all that is small stuff. Dad and I will handle it. You need to take care of yourself. This is huge for you. But you know, after Annie's experience with Michael's suicide, this isn't life or death, is it?"

"You're right, Mom. But I feel so betrayed. Why couldn't he have told me before? We were together for over six years. Didn't that mean anything to him?"

"I don't know, Sara, but he's obviously a weak guy who doesn't deserve you."

Sara crawled into bed and I sat at the kitchen table, angry but determined to do the best I could. Ric called me that evening. "How's it going?"

"You won't believe this."

After insisting it not be at our house, we held a party there after all for our friends and family. The food had already been paid for, motel rooms were rented, plane tickets were purchased.

I made a million phone calls before Ric returned the following night. I didn't have time to worry about how the house and yard looked. I booked a two-night's stay for Sara at a spa in Calistoga. Over the weekend Annie would stay with her one night, and I, the next night after our guests left. We made one big mistake: Sara tried to disappear into her room during the party. Way too many people insisted on talking to her and giving her consoling advice. Good intentions, bad results. Sara was a quivering mess by the time Annie drove her north that evening.

Truthfully, I remember nothing about Jenna during the entire debacle. I assume she stood to the side, silent. Perhaps Ric's dad took care of her. My mind was on my firstborn. It seemed that in the four years Jenna had been with us we had suffered one catastrophe after another having nothing to do with her. I was relieved my mental health was steady and under control.

18

Challenge Day

A program developed by a married couple in nearby Concord in the late 1980s, Challenge Day came early to the Martinez schools. I participated as a volunteer when Annie was in seventh grade and thought it was an excellent method for teaching kids tolerance. The program has since been used all over the US and internationally. Even Oprah was a fan and featured the founders on her show.

Over the course of the day, students and adults build trust by playing games within the whole group and by sharing confidences in small groups. It helps break down barriers among students. They begin to realize that each of them has issues and hardships and that treating each other with kindness and respect makes for a better school environment and world.

Cross the Line, an activity that took place near the end of the day, had a big impact on me the day I volunteered. In silence, all students and adults stood behind a line made of tape on the floor. Challenge Day trainers called out experiences. Everyone who matched a particular experience crossed over the line and turned to face the others, always in silence. They then returned and joined the entire group. Each statement began "Cross over the line if you have ever …" Some examples were benign: "… if you have ever played sports; if you're left-handed; if you have a stepparent." More were emotional and troubling: "… if you have ever had an eating disorder; if you have ever been the target of a racist comment; if you have had someone you love affected by alcoholism; if you, a friend, or a family member has been abused."

One of the last statements was "Cross over the line if you have never been a child." I scrunched my eyebrows and thought, *How can anyone have never been a child?* Three people crossed the line: two adults and an eighth-grader, Max. I was perplexed. The Challenge Day leader asked if anyone would like to talk about their reasons.

Max, a known bully at school, said, "I always had to protect my mom from men who hit her. I never got to be a child." All of us remained quiet as we dispersed into our small groups in order to debrief the day. I thought about Max and how he had had to develop a hard shell to deal with his pain.

I walked away from the event impressed with Challenge Day. I followed the organization's success and got involved with it again when I worked at Olympic. One year another teacher and I worked hard to find adults who would agree to become mentors to each of all twenty-five participating students. As hard as it was to organize, several of those mentor matches flourished for years.

In seventh grade Jenna participated in Challenge Day. Signing the permission slip, I hoped she would be affected in a positive way. It was worth a try. I didn't volunteer that time; my involvement would certainly make Jenna uncomfortable.

The evening after the event, I asked her how she liked it. She said it was okay. The next afternoon was a different story. When I picked her up from school and she climbed into the car, she burst into tears.

"What's the matter, Jenna?"

"I don't want to talk about it." We were silent as we drove home. She went straight to her room and shut the door.

A half hour later I knocked on her door.

"Jenna, do you want to talk now?"

"I guess so," she said quietly. I opened the door thinking, *Wow, this is different. She actually wants to talk to me.*

Jenna said, "Today was horrible, all because of Challenge Day."

"What happened?"

"I told my group a secret and people spread it all over school. The boys called me easy and a slut while they laughed and shoved each other."

"Why?"

Jenna looked down at her bedspread. She spoke in a whisper. "I never told you, but when I was little …" She paused and I put my arm around her. She didn't recoil. "Do you know about Cross the Line?"

"I do," I said. "It's very powerful."

She looked sideways at me and then down. "When we returned to our small group, I told them my mom let men do things to me when I was five. All of us agreed to keep everything in confidence, but it leaked out at school. I don't ever want to go back."

I cringed. Crystal was a horrific person, but to let men abuse her child? I couldn't have been more appalled. I imagined the scenario: in exchange for drugs or money she let men have at it with this poor innocent child. The thought of what she did and what might have been done to

Jenna made me nauseous. Crystal truly was evil.

I squeezed Jenna tightly and she actually hugged me back. "I am so sorry. I had no idea. Staying at home isn't the answer, though. I think you should go back to school tomorrow and ignore all those horrible boys. I'm sure they'll forget about it if you don't react."

She leaned into me and hung her head. "I don't know if I can do it, Aunt Alice."

"Yes, you can. And I'll make sure you'll be okay." Inside I had no idea if I could fulfill my promise, but I planned to call the school counselor, a man I trusted, in the morning. My positive impression of Challenge Day had died. At the very least, immature seventh-graders were too young to participate in such an emotional experience.

Within a week Jenna acted as if nothing had happened. She locked up her feelings again. I couldn't imagine that she might have made up something so abhorrent. Or had she? Getting attention was what Jenna wanted, whether positive or negative. Maybe she got caught up in the moment of the emotional day and wanted others to feel sorry for her. I was sure the aftermath at school wasn't what she expected, but I had no idea if what she had divulged was true or not. I wouldn't put it past her to lie, or past her mother to have really done it.

19

North Woods Adventure

Jenna often took passive-aggressive behavior to the extreme. She had an amazing ability to look directly at you, agree to whatever you were asking of her, and then do exactly nothing toward accomplishing it. She exasperated Ric and me to no end, but on one occasion she outdid even herself.

During the summer before she turned twelve, I devised a way to give Ric and myself a needed vacation and Jenna an experience of a lifetime. My cousin's daughter Sue and her husband, Andy, owned an outfitting resort in the Boundary Waters Canoe Area Wilderness in Minnesota near the Canadian border. We had camped with them in the area five years before they bought their business, Tuscarora Outfitters, and I couldn't wait to see their place. I called Sue and asked her if she knew of any nearby summer camps for kids. Pausing only seconds, she told me about Camp Menogyn, a YMCA program that seemed perfect for Jenna. We could enjoy a week of peace in a small cabin at Sue's rustic resort while Jenna tested herself in the wilderness of the North Woods. She would spend the first night in a cabin enjoying traditional camp activities and then take off with five other girls and a counselor for four days of roughing it with canoes and minimal camping gear. Kind of an Outward Bound experience for kids her age.

Jenna wasn't happy about the plan, but a small-world experience at Olympic High School made it a little more palatable to her. When I mentioned our plan to Rinda, my new principal, she exclaimed "Camp Menogyn! I was a counselor there. That place literally changed my life." The next time Rinda saw Jenna she began singing the camp song to her …

> *The life of a voyager*
> *That of a sojourner*
> *Traveling around and round*
> *But not from town to town*

Travels the lakes and streams
Follows his distant dreams
Peace on the waterway
Blue sky and cloudy day

My heart has just one home
From which I'll never roam
Land of true happiness
Canadian wilderness

The call of the lonely loon
Coyotes howling at the moon
Wind rustling through the trees
That's a Canadian breeze

"Jenna, you'll just love Camp Menogyn. I spent five summers there and loved every minute. The last two years I was a counselor. It's beautiful, and everyone there is super friendly. When you're in the dining room, be sure to look for my name on one of the canoe paddles on the wall. I bet it's still there."

Jenna smiled but didn't say anything. I hoped Rinda's enthusiasm would rub off on her.

As summer got closer, we received loads of correspondence from the camp. Brochures showed photos of smiling kids, dense woods, loons, eagles, moose, and sparkling lakes. Included in the mail were lists and reminders of everything

Jenna should pack for the week. The things she didn't already have, we purchased. I marked all her clothing with her name as the camp suggested.

When I was her age, my sister, Pam, and I went to a horse camp in the mountains behind Santa Barbara. I had great memories of Rancho Oso and told Jenna about some of them. "One year," I told her, "I was assigned a horse named Chico. He was a gentle Indian paint horse, white with brown patches. We learned how to care for our horses and rode every day. We fed them, brushed them, took care of their saddles and bridles, and cleaned out their stalls. At the end of the week we had a little horse show when our parents came to pick us up."

I was lost in my memories while Jenna sat there, silent. She wasn't a tomboy like I had been and didn't enjoy spending time outdoors, but I hoped she'd love the camp once she got there.

On the flight to Duluth I was relaxed and happy. I couldn't imagine a more perfect vacation than a week in the Boundary Waters. Ric and I planned to stay in one of Sue and Andy's cabins on Round Lake. We looked forward to paddling a canoe in the nearby lakes and spending time with a friendly family. Their kids, Shelby and Danny, had moved to Tuscarora when they were young and were very much at home in the wilderness. They commuted with eight other children fifty miles each way on the school bus to the small town of Grand Marais. In the winter months they spent the night with "townies" if the weather was too severe. They thrived. Ten-year-old Danny was becoming quite the fishing guide and Shelby, thirteen, loved helping the college kids who worked at the resort.

While we flew over the plains of Nebraska, I had a terrible thought. "Jenna, I don't remember you carrying your sleeping bag to the airport." No response. "Did you pack your heavy jacket?" She stared at me.

I closed my eyes, took a deep breath and exhaled. I guessed Jenna had decided the best way to avoid Camp Menogyn was to happen to forget to pack many of the things on the camp list. I imagined her thinking to herself, *That way I won't have to go. They'll send me home.*

I was outraged. "I can't believe you did this. And if you think for one minute this will get you out of going to camp, think again. As soon as we get to Duluth we're going to find a store, buy what you left at home, and add up the bill."

Ric joined me. "You'll pay us back in extra chores for everything we buy."

I steamed. She looked out the window.

We found a Kmart, loaded up our cart with camp supplies, and drove the four hours to Camp Menogyn. The northern limits of Duluth along the shores of Lake Superior were lined with stately homes from the days when iron ore was king. Their gardens were filled with the tallest, most colorful lupines I'd ever seen; pink, blue, purple, yellow, orange, and white. Jenna was quiet in the back seat, and I did my best to focus on the drive. Lake Superior is the famous Gitche Gumee of Hiawatha fame, and the few words I remembered floated through my mind as we drove along the lake: "By the shores of Gitche Gumme, by the shining big sea water, stood Nokomis, the old woman."

We passed quaint small towns, state parks, waterfalls, campgrounds, lighthouses, red rock mountains, and dark green forests. The scenery was a wonderful distraction. Once we got to Grand Marais, we turned inland on the Gun-flint Trail highway. Its name made me think of the French-Canadian voyageurs who explored the lake-filled region by canoe and foot in the eighteenth and nineteenth centuries.

The Kmart stop made us late. By the time we arrived at the camp, everyone was waiting for us. Most kids came by bus from Minneapolis. Jenna's group made a big deal of her arrival, cheering and singing the camp song Rinda had taught us. Jenna was smiling and seemed happy. I turned to Ric. "Let's get out while the getting's good."

We left Jenna in capable hands and enjoyed a few more miles of the wooded Gunflint Trail before turning into the dirt driveway of Tuscarora Outfitters. As we negotiated the narrow road, we saw a small pond to our right. We stopped. Evening mist was rising from the water, and on the edge were a mother and baby moose. We gazed at the ungainly animals and smiled at each other.

"Ricky B, this week is going to be amazing."

We found Sue in the resort's small store, bent over fishing supplies and boxes of T-shirts.

"Just in time, you two," she said when she saw us, grinning. "You can help me."

Hugs all around. She showed us to our cabin, and we spent the hour before dinner exploring the resort. In addition to six small cabins, Tuscarora had bunkhouses for overnighters before they took off on their canoeing adventures. It also had a dining room and kitchen, a large supply building, and a map room for customers to plan their trips. Two large vans with racks were parked next to the supply building, and canoes were stacked in the grass. A small dock and beach fronted Round Lake and the forest around it. On the opposite side was the edge of the official wilderness area where no structures were allowed. Trails led from lake to lake. Canoers portaged between lakes: they carried canoes on their shoulders with heavy packs on their backs and/or fronts. Made for the area, they were known as Duluth Packs. In our case, all we had to carry was a canoe.

After dinner in the dining hall with Sue's family and the staff, we watched the sun go down and went to bed early, anxious to get out on the lake in the morning.

At seven thirty the next morning, Sue knocked on our cabin door.

"There is a phone call for you from the Menogyn camp director."

My heart skipped a beat, certain our hopes for a carefree week were going to flush down the drain.

"Last night I was afraid I was going to have to ask you to pick Jenna up this morning," the camp director said. "She was very unhappy and told us she refused to stay. Now I'm calling with good news. I'm watching her and her group paddle away from the camp. She is smiling ear to ear. Her counselor worked magic on her."

With relief, we ate breakfast and took off in our canoe. We paddled all around the small lake. Among some large rocks near the far-side shore, we found a family of ducks: mom and a dozen tiny, fuzzy, yellow-and-brown ducklings. She jumped from a large rock into the water, and each duckling followed her, some more quickly than others. We could practically hear them: "Mom, wait up!"

By the time we got back, Sue's retired parents, my cousin Jane and her husband, Sheldon, had arrived. They were in another cabin, and, as they had the previous summer, were there to help Sue and Andy for the season. Sue also hired several college students; she was in her element as a former teacher. They maintained the camping food and equipment room, kept the bunkhouses clean, and worked in the dining room. Andy was an expert at helping guests plan their trips in the map room. He hauled trailers loaded with canoes to nearby lakes where the groups chose to begin their adventures and picked them up on their return.

I had already heard stories from two people about how important it was to keep a map close at hand when canoeing there. The first principal I worked for at Olympic, Marcie, spent part of her honeymoon in the Boundary Waters. She and her new husband were from Chicago and had never been there before. They rented a little lakeside cabin that came with a dock and a canoe. The first morning they paddled and paddled, admiring the beautiful islands, woods, and wildlife. After a couple of hours they realized they were lost; everything looked the same. They didn't panic, but it was five hours before they rounded an island and spied their cabin.

When I told my dad we were going to visit Sue and Andy, he had a similar story to tell. He and some of his college buddies drove north from the University of Wisconsin, a long day's journey. They left their gear onshore and took two canoes out for a paddle. When darkness was imminent, they found themselves lost. They continued until it was too dark to see, then pulled into shore and decided to wait out the night. They had no matches, no blankets, no food. They spent a miserable night and then, as it got light, they looked across a narrow channel only to see their car and camping gear.

I resolved to be diligent. Every time Ric and I took a canoe out, I was very careful to hold a map in my lap and to constantly look for landmarks. The map was waterproof and detailed, and it helped that I was good at reading maps. And we never got lost.

We had an exciting, fun week. During the day we paddled amid spectacular scenery. Woods of spruce, fir, and pine, and shrubbery including ripe blueberries and raspberries, were so thick it was impossible to walk off-trail. Wildlife was at every turn: beaver, loons, eagles, deer, otters, and moose. Catching pike and walleye was exciting for Ric. We spent time with my three generations of cousins in the evenings; it was wonderful to be with a happy family. Danny, in an entrepreneurial spirit, sold me two trivets he made from slices of a birch tree limb. He had burned "Tuscarora" on them with a small wood-burning tool.

We didn't hear from the camp director again, so we assumed all was good with Jenna. When we picked her up, we were astonished. She was giggly and eager to show us her hundreds of mosquito bites and newfound skills. Back at Sue and Andy's, she couldn't wait to flip a two-person metal canoe up and over her shoulders and carry it. During the night I thought about returning the following year and wondered how long her positive attitude would last.

The answer: exactly twenty-four hours. By the time we reached the airport in Duluth, she was the same sullen girl we'd known before. This was yet another failed attempt to jolt Jenna into understanding she could be someone other than the victim of a wretched childhood. I was disappointed yet again, but we were in this for the long haul. Ric and I would give her our best until she was eighteen. If, by that time, she still didn't want to act like a member of our family, she would be free to live a life she would make for herself. Six-plus years to go.

20

Anticipating the Worst

Jenna didn't change in her interactions with us during the next three years, from age eleven until she began high school at fourteen. We had glimpses of improvements, like the EMDR therapy that helped her let go of her traumatic fear of Alan, her brother Brandon's father. But after each glimpse she reverted to her normal behavior: continually sullen and uncommunicative; untrustworthy; a poor student; undemonstrative. Her visits with Crystal were infrequent, and too many times Jenna waited in vain for her mother to call or show up. The gatherings with her siblings two or three times a year, always arranged by her Grandpa Bob, became strained.

Her brother Brandon made life miserable for his foster parents. Willful and violent, he later spent his teenage years in and out of group homes and told Jenna he wanted to be just like his dad, the vicious meth addict and dealer who had tortured her. Their little sister, Leticia, had a happy life with her foster mom in a stable home. Removing her from Crystal as an infant meant she had no lasting memories of the abuse and trauma her stepbrother and sister carried. She hardly knew her siblings, who tended to gang up on her. Early on, when she was three or four, I saw them point toward her foster mother and tell her, "She's not really your mom."

Thankful for the skills I learned in the Parent Project class, Ric and I were able to control our emotions. We used TEASPOT (take everything away for a short period of time) regularly. If she broke one of our household rules, we took away the things she enjoyed. It wasn't particularly successful since she held few things dear, but we continued to implement it.

Sara and Annie felt bad about the burden Jenna placed on us. We explained to them we had no regrets. Raising Jenna was our responsibility, and we accepted her troubles and obstacles. Between our years of experience and the ability to work as a strong team, in some ways raising Jenna proved easier than raising our daughters had been, but parenting her left us mentally exhausted.

Jenna gravitated toward kids who were from broken homes or who lived in poverty. I tried hard to be open-minded and nonjudgmental. Truly, the girls who spent time at our house were very nice, but it unnerved me to drop Jenna off at a motel-turned-apartment or a home where countless people resided. I understood why she picked these girls, but I was out of my element: a mirror of how she must have felt in our world.

Annie transferred to Sacramento City College when Jenna was ten, finished her undergraduate studies at Sacramento State University, and completed a teaching credential program there. When she was home on occasional weekends, she kept a watchful eye on Jenna.

Like most young people, Annie knew a lot more about computers than Ric and I did. One day she called from the loft. "Mom, do you know who Jenna has been chatting with on the Internet? You're not going to believe this."

I trudged upstairs. Annie had a stack of papers in her hand and gave them to me. She had gone through Jenna's email history and found multiple conversations with someone from Philadelphia. As I read the printed copies, my stomach sank. At fourteen she had a cyberspace love affair fully in the works and planned to meet a guy named Mack at the Oakland Airport in two weeks.

"I can't believe it," I said. "This is just like what you read in the papers. God knows who this Mack person is. He could be a sex trafficker or a murderer. Now that I think about it, I confronted Jenna with our phone bill last month. There were several expensive calls to Philadelphia. She told me a new friend from school recently moved to Martinez from there. Without missing a beat she said, 'Sorry, she must still have her old cell phone.' Another split-second lie. And I believed her. What a nightmare. I feel like such a fool."

"You're not a fool, Mom. You're a kindhearted person who has been going over the top for Jenna for too many years. Don't beat yourself up."

I thought for a moment. "I'm going to show these printouts to Jenna, then do the TEASPOT thing. If you hadn't unearthed this, I can only imagine what would have happened."

I didn't expect much of a reaction when I confronted Jenna. After I showed her the evidence, she stared at me with her big, brown, emotionless eyes and said nothing. I took a breath, counted to ten, and sent her to her room without TV for a week.

With Jenna in high school, I became concerned about what she might do with unsupervised time. She had at least an hour after school before I picked her up. Our town had no school buses and lacked convenient public transportation. She didn't enjoy sports, and there were no other supervised after-school programs. She told me she either hung out with friends or did homework in the library, but I really didn't know.

Until now Jenna had been passive, but I foresaw serious trouble ahead. We weren't equipped with the skills, patience, or energy to tolerate an out-of-control teenager. I began to research therapeutic boarding schools. Perhaps they could work the magic we couldn't. I first looked online and was dismayed as I read about schools that were not what they advertised: children were given harsh, ineffective "treatment"; they were isolated from their families and had minimal contact; and they received substandard education.

I racked my brain and called Manny, the school psychologist who co-taught the Parent Project and had recommended Jenna's therapist, Linda. I knew him fairly well, liked him, and trusted his judgment. He had an immediate suggestion.

"A friend who has been a child social worker for years recently opened his own practice. Guy specializes in helping teens who have completed their stays at boarding schools. Adjusting to home life is often very difficult for them, and his service is needed. He worked with many schools both in and out of California in his previous county job."

Given Jenna's background and behaviors, she

qualified as having an emotional disability under special education criteria. That meant she met regularly with school psychologists and had done so since third grade. As a school board member, I had occasionally approved transfer requests for children who were physically or mentally disabled. Care outside our district was expensive; even in 1995, ten years earlier, the cost was $30,000 to $70,000 per year. We weren't sure if our school district would approve and pay for such a move, but I wanted to have a plan in place in case we needed that option.

When I visited Guy, Manny's friend, he impressed me with his knowledge and easygoing personality. He told me he knew of some good schools out of state that were relatively afford-able. After listening to me describe Jenna's and our family's history, he suggested that Rancho Valmora, a school east of Santa Fe, New Mexico, might be a good fit for her. He had placed teens there when he was a social worker. He regularly checked on them in person and found it to be an honest, caring, professional institution.

I wanted to be prepared in case it became necessary for us to seek this kind of help. It would be a drastic change, but we didn't feel Jenna was making progress under our care. Guy said he would be happy to help us in the future. I tucked that information away.

21

No Surprise

Jenna went to weekly sessions with her therapist, Linda, for a year and a half. I didn't know the details of what they talked about since their conversations were confidential, but I felt the meetings were much more productive than those during the three years she spent with Grace McMahon. Jenna was experienced at telling people exactly what they wanted to hear, never revealing her true feelings. Linda was adept at distinguishing truth from fiction and called her on it. I think Jenna respected her for that. The success of the EMDR sessions was quite remarkable. As a result, they seemed to have an open, trusting relationship, or at least as honest as Jenna could make it.

In addition to being beaten down from the abuse she had suffered, Jenna continually sabotaged herself and was forever the victim. Her blank, empty stare was scary. Remorse was not in her nature. How could there be such emptiness in a person's soul? This aspect of Jenna's personality always gnawed at me. Many of my Olympic students had something in them that shouted, "I'm going to be somebody! I'm not going to let my background determine my future!" Why was there such a difference? It was like there was a big void in Jenna's being. Nothing there.

Her therapy sessions were on Tuesday afternoons from 5 to 6 o'clock. Commute traffic between Martinez and Alamo was most often bad. By the time we arrived at Linda's office, I was happy to sit in the waiting room by myself, reading.

One day, in spring 2005 when Jenna was fourteen, the door opened after half an hour.

Linda came out. "Jenna has something she wants to share with you."

That was a first. My heart skipped with trepidation, not knowing what was coming. Usually she and I traveled in near silence to and from the sessions. Most teenagers find conversing with their parents abhorrent, and she was no exception. I never pushed it, having already raised two girls.

Jenna slumped in her chair and avoided eye contact. After a lengthy silence in which she seemed to pull herself together, she spoke. "Do you remember when you picked me up last Tuesday, and I was sitting in front of that guy's house next to the high school?"

I remembered. Jenna called me from the school's office phone to ask me to pick her up there instead of in front of the school.

"I wasn't just waiting in front of his house," she said. "He and I had sex before that." She looked at me with daring in her eyes.

I spoke before I could think of the best response. "Do you think I'm surprised, Jenna? I'm very disappointed and concerned for you, but surprised? No. I have very little influence on what you do. I just hope you're using protection and aren't giving your body to someone you don't have strong feelings for."

Silence. Linda broke in. "Jenna didn't want to hide this from you."

Likely story, I thought. *Instead, she was probably hoping for some shock value from her admission.* My response wasn't the most caring, but I was beyond that.

"I appreciate that, but like I said, I'm really not surprised. Having sex at fourteen is much too young in my mind. I worry about your self-esteem and future relationships, Jenna. You have a lifetime ahead of you. Please be careful. What you do might have everlasting consequences."

I thought of the advice I had received when Jenna was a young girl: providing her a safe, warm family environment was as much as I could hope to do. Those words helped me get through many trying times. This was one more of them.

There seemed nothing left to say, so I excused myself and waited for the session to end.

22

On Her Way

Jenna visited her Grandpa Bob at least twice a year. Our routine was to meet him on I-5 at the Olive Pit store and restaurant in Corning. He developed a serious case of bone cancer when she was thirteen, but it didn't affect the visits. Shortly after Jenna turned fourteen, Bob looked particularly drawn and pale. I was worried about him but wasn't prepared for his request.

"I wonder if you two would consider allowing Jenna to have a special hardship driver's license," he said. "As I understand it, in special circumstances fourteen-year-olds can receive a restricted license. In our case, it would be to drive with me.

My eyesight is going bad, and it's more difficult for me to drive."

My first thought: *Preposterous—what is he thinking?*

Ric met my eyes and then turned to Bob. "We'll have to talk it over, Bob. That's something we've never heard of."

After we got home and were alone, we discussed it. I said, "I can't believe what Bob is suggesting. What, have Jenna drive him all the way both ways, or worse, have him meet us halfway in his semi-blindness? None of it makes any sense. Besides, the very last thing Jenna should be doing is learning to drive a car."

"I agree," said Ric. "I sure hope he hasn't let her practice already."

On a Saturday a few weeks later, Ric and I were awake but not yet up in the funky little trailer we used on our weekend retreats in Boonville. A huffing diesel vehicle made its way up our driveway. Ric jumped up and pulled on a pair of jeans. Before he had time to put on a shirt, we heard a door slam, footsteps, and whistling. It had to be our good friend Wally from Boonville. He was the only person I knew other than me who whistled all the time.

"Hey, are you guys awake?" he called out. "Sara phoned and said she needs you to call home. Something about Jenna taking your truck."

I rolled over and hid my head under the pillow. *Oh, no.* As Ric and Wally talked outside, I pushed the pillow away, got dressed, kicked open the warped door of the trailer, and joined them by Wally's truck. "Tell me what happened."

"I'm not exactly sure," said Wally, "but apparently both Ric's truck and Jenna are missing."

We had no phone service on our property, and that was the way we liked it. Ric wore two pagers from the refinery, one for general calls and one for emergencies. When he wasn't on call and could escape to our retreat, he loved nothing better than when his pager read "out of range." Our girls knew to call Wally and Sue if they needed to reach us, but this was the first time they'd had to do it. Wally got back into his truck and left. Ric and I looked at one another.

"Let's make coffee, grab some cereal, and hit the road," I said. "No sense worrying until we know exactly what's going on. We can call from down the hill when we get cell service." My mind reeled, wondering what we'd find out and what we'd do next. Ric didn't say anything, but I knew his brain was also churning.

Sara answered after the first ring. "What happened?" I asked.

"I'm so sorry, Mom. I went to a baseball game and told Jenna I'd be home by ten last night. When I got back, she was gone and so was Dad's truck. First, I looked all over the house, worried something had happened to her. Then I called the police and Annie. She got here from Sacramento a few minutes after the police did. We wanted to report the truck stolen, but they talked us out of it because Jenna was family. Annie drove all over town looking for her while I waited, hoping she'd return. Neither of us slept. Right after we called Wally this morning, I walked to the end of the driveway to get the paper. The truck was parked in the cul-de-sac. The driver's side was creased like it had scraped a guardrail. There was no Jenna. We're guessing she returned it and was too scared to come into the house. When will you be home?"

I told her we were leaving Boonville and would be home in two and a half hours. I was furious, and Ric's anger made him less than careful driving curvy Highway 128. Once we got to the freeway in Cloverdale, I said to Ric, "That does it. I think we should send Jenna to one of the therapeutic boarding schools the counselor, Guy, told me about. I'm not going to live like this."

Ric's cell phone tooted its bugle ring. I answered. It was Annie. She told us what happened after we'd last talked with Sara. Jenna's friend Vanessa came to our house looking for a coat she'd left behind. Sara and Annie virtually kidnapped her, forcing her to tell them where Jenna was. Vanessa cried and said Jenna was at the nearby Safeway. She left, and the girls got into Sara's PT Cruiser and drove down Virginia Hills Drive to the shopping center. Jenna wasn't there. They drove toward downtown Martinez on Alhambra Avenue, a wide thoroughfare. A mile away they came upon Jenna and a scruffy teenage boy walking alongside the road. Sara screeched to a halt in front of the pair. Annie threw the door open and yelled, "Get in!" The boy ran away. Jenna slid into the back seat. She was wearing a short skirt, a low-cut shirt, and no shoes; she carried high heels. She had a gigantic hickey on her neck. Her face was a mess with running mascara and thick makeup.

Annie screamed at Jenna. Sara was beyond angry and was ready to kill her when Annie called Ric. After a minute's explanation, she turned the phone over to Jenna. I pictured her sitting stone-faced. He raged at her while I held his arm and motioned him to calm him down. The last thing we needed was for him to be pulled over for talking on his phone while driving.

23

J Ward

Jenna stole Ric's truck shortly after school ended for the summer. Although my work year spanned eleven months, through June, my principal allowed me to stay home to deal with Jenna and make up my work later. I called Guy and asked him to find out when Rancho Valmora or a similar school might have an opening for her. She wasn't aware of our plans to take her there.

A week later Ric took off for our nephew Tim's bachelor party in the San Juan Islands. Our whole family was invited to attend his wedding celebration on Orcas Island, and I wasn't going to miss it. My parents were too elderly to travel, but my sister, Pam, and our Aunt Ione planned to fly with the girls and me from Oakland to Seattle, catch a shuttle to the Anacortes ferry, and take the hour-long ride to Orcas. We were still livid with Jenna, but we had purchased her airline ticket weeks before and thought it was important she join our larger family for the special event. I definitely wanted her under my thumb.

In the interim I followed TEASPOT. For a week, the longest effective period according to the training, Jenna had no phone or TV privileges, no music, and no contact with friends. School was out, and she mostly did what she was best at: waiting and doing nothing. In her passive-aggressive way, she showed little response to our absolute outrage at what she'd done.

The afternoon before we were to leave for Washington, I took Jenna to her weekly counseling appointment with Linda. She knew Jenna had taken the truck; I had phoned her right after it had happened. I wasn't privy to their conversation, but I hoped Linda was helping Jenna understand the seriousness of what she had done. She was in a somber mood when we left Linda's office.

On the way home, my mind focused on the hours ahead. Pam and Ione arrived that afternoon, their beds were set up, and I had asked Sara to pick up a pizza. I planned to get up at 5:00 a.m. Our flight left early so we would have time to attend a dinner with our immediate family that evening. Traffic was stop and go between Danville and Walnut Creek. Tired and irritated, I ignored Jenna.

Out of the blue she said, "I feel like I want to hurt myself."

My head whirled toward her. "You feel like you want to do what?"

"Hurt myself." She looked at the floor.

"Do you know what you're saying? What that means I have to do if you're serious?" No response.

"If you mean you feel suicidal, it means I have to take you to the psychiatric ward at the hospital." Again, no response. She stared out the window.

My blood pressure surged. What more would this girl do to push my buttons? There was no way she had the courage to kill herself. She lacked the will, the inner strength. This seemed to be yet another way for her to wreck plans and distance herself from our family. I drove in silence, stewing. Traffic on I-680 started to move as the lanes widened from two to three. I passed our home exit and headed toward downtown Martinez.

"Okay. I'm taking you to J Ward at County Hospital." My mind made up, I pressed my foot to the floor. We exited at Pacheco Avenue and I slowed to fifty miles an hour, five faster than the limit. Halfway to downtown I broke the dreadful silence. I turned and yelled at Jenna. "Why don't you save us a lot of trouble and throw yourself out the door?" Jenna froze. I rarely raised my voice.

I continued to drive furiously. I pulled into the county hospital and marched inside. Jenna followed. We entered the psychiatric ward. I had heard about the infamous J Ward for crazy people but had never been there. It was dim, silent. I guess I expected to hear screaming and ranting. I remembered reading about escapees who wandered about downtown Martinez, frightening people but generally drugged and meek. We passed darkened cubicles as we headed to the receptionist's desk. Jenna hung back. A strong antiseptic odor pervaded the room.

I explained my purpose to the intake woman, and after I answered a few questions she said, "You say you have Kaiser insurance? Then you need to go to a Kaiser hospital. They'll treat her there."

I gazed at her, shaking my head. *Why didn't I think of that?* Distraught, I grabbed Jenna's arm and hauled her back to the car, limp as a rag doll. We backtracked to the nearest Kaiser facility, in Walnut Creek not far from Linda's office.

On top of Jenna's issues, our houseguests were worrisome: Pam wore an eye patch for her temporary Bell's Palsy; Ione, in her mid-eighties, was nearly deaf. The trip to Orcas Island would be taxing, if we ever made it there. It was already past 7 p.m.

I called the girls from the hospital emergency room to let them know our whereabouts and flopped into a chair. Jenna sat next to me but stared straight ahead. An hour went by before we were taken to an examining cubicle. I thumbed through magazines while Jenna did nothing. Another forty-five minutes passed. Finally, a nurse appeared and a young doctor followed. I glanced at my watch: 9:15. I asked to talk to the doctor alone and told him about Jenna as succinctly as I could. I also told him about our trip. He told me they would normally hold a person for a seventy-two-hour waiting period, but given her situation, they would probably transfer her to a juvenile mental health facility and keep her there until we returned. I wanted to hug him.

I drove home, said my hellos, gobbled a slice of pizza, and went to bed. Five a.m. came much too soon. Our trip was arduous. Handling luggage and going through security were complicated by my travel mates: two twenty-somethings, my ill sister, and my eighty-four-year-old aunt. On the ferry to Orcas I sat on a bench, eyes burning. Despite the ordeal, relief was my foremost emotion. A carefree, long weekend awaited us while

Jenna remained in good hands. A load of stress fell from my shoulders.

We exited the ferry in a thick drizzle. The girls and I schlepped our luggage across the street, only to find that there no place to wait. A narrow awning in front of a stationery store provided our only cover. I had called Ric from Anacortes but didn't tell him about Jenna. All in good time. Expecting him to pick us up momentarily, we squeezed together and waited. And waited. I peered down the waterfront and a small VW Golf finally pulled up. A grizzled-faced Ric rolled his window down, grinned, and said, "Hi!" My cousin Hugh was in the passenger seat. It would be difficult to fit three people in the rear, much less five of us and our bags.

"Is someone bringing another car?" I asked.

"Nope. Everyone else is busy. I thought we could make two trips."

Obviously still buoyant from his week of debauchery on Puget Sound, he continued to smile like a goof. I blinked. "Are you kidding me? The girls and I are supposed to wait in the rain until you return?" The virtual rope I was hanging on to was unravelling. At my very wit's end, I needed a hot shower, a tumbler full of gin, and a nap, in that order. "You have no idea what I've been through, and I'm not about to tell you now. Get out of here and hurry back."

Ric looked confused as I stormed away, but he dutifully loaded up Pam and Ione and took off down the road.

Annie and Sara each took an arm and led me to a bench under the awning. "It's all right, Mom," Sara said. "It'll be okay and we'll have a wonderful time."

"I know, but I'm not sure how much more I can take before I blow." I stared at the ocean. And waited.

24

Off to Las Vegas

The weeks went by quickly after Jenna was admitted to Kaiser Hospital in Walnut Creek. She was transferred to a juvenile mental health facility in Vallejo before we returned from Washington. Tuesday, Ric and I drove to visit Jenna. On the way, we talked about our next steps.

"Remember Rancho Valmora, the school I heard about from the teen specialist I talked to? He said there will be an opening shortly."

"I remember. Where is it again?"

"In New Mexico east of Santa Fe."

Ric said, "Are you sure that's what we should do right away?"

"I've spent months researching therapeutic

boarding schools. There are a lot of sketchy ones where kids are mistreated, but I feel good about Rancho Valmora. Guy has placed kids there with good results. It's much less expensive than California schools, and I'm not positive the school district will pick up the cost. I just don't want to wait any longer."

"You're probably right. The next stunt Jenna pulls might hurt her or someone else. I still can't believe she drove my truck all the way to Richmond with those punks," said Ric.

He turned into the parking lot in front of the Kaiser building. It was nondescript and dated. We registered at the front desk and looked around. With its low ceilings and small rooms, I guessed it was built in the 1950s. The walls were painted a light olive green, and it smelled of disinfectant. Upholstered chairs in the waiting room were torn and stained.

A therapist ushered us into a small office and went to get Jenna. She arrived in sweats and slip-on canvas shoes. Her hair was tightly braided in the "gangsta" style popular with urban teenagers. My eyes widened and I blinked, but I said nothing except, "Hello, Jenna." I hugged her and we sat down.

Jenna avoided looking at us. The counselor explained the daily schedule, which included both group and individual therapy. We walked to the room assigned to Jenna. It reminded me of a college dorm, with two twin beds and small dressers, but without desks or windows.

"Do you have a roommate?" I asked.

"Yeah."

It was obvious she didn't want to talk to us. We left her in the group area and walked with the therapist to her office, where we explained Jenna's history, our relationship with her, and the situation that brought her to the facility. We also told her we planned to move Jenna to a therapeutic boarding school as soon as we could.

"I think that's an excellent plan," she said. "Jenna is a very troubled young woman who needs a lot of therapy."

After ten days, the Kaiser staff thought her immediate needs would be better met at a teen psychiatric ward at Alta Bates Hospital in Berkeley. We were jubilant the powers that be saw her condition as seriously as we did. This girl was in dire need of full-time professional help. The psychiatrist at Alta Bates was supportive and direct.

"As soon as that school has a place for Jenna," she said, "I want you to come here and take her directly there. Don't tell her anything about it beforehand. Just pack some clothes for her, pick her up, and take her to the airport."

Walking out of the hospital, I felt lighter than I had in years. Finally, people other than Ric and

I were going to be responsible for Jenna. I looked forward to her receiving the help we couldn't give her. I also looked forward to visiting her in New Mexico. We had visited the Land of Enchantment several times before and found it to be fascinating.

The school was located near a small town named Las Vegas. We had no need to gamble on this venture. It was out of our hands.

Three weeks later, in July 2005, we picked Jenna up at 5:30 a.m. prior to our flight from Oakland to Albuquerque. In typical fashion, Jenna showed no emotion when we told her where we were going. I guess it made it easier than if she'd gone screaming and kicking, but her attitude was always so strange, so atypical of teenagers. She remained silent throughout the trip, which I expected.

The flight was uneventful. I had used a list the staff from Rancho Valmora provided to pack for Jenna. I included two things she treasured: a "quillow" her mother gave her—a quilt that folded into a pillow—and a large photo of her and her mother. She had received the original small picture from her Grandpa Bob. It was bent and cracked; I'd had it enlarged and restored to take with her.

Ric and I had been to northern New Mexico, but we'd never been in the eastern part of the state. Interstate 25 led northeast from Albuquerque and turned east at Santa Fe. We climbed out of the dry Rio Grande Valley and began to see forests of ponderosa pine, juniper, and scrubby pinon pine. At the high point, Glorieta Pass, we noticed road signs for the town of Pecos and Pecos National Historical Park.

"Pecos," I said. "I thought that was a river in Texas. Maybe we could stop there for lunch."

We took the exit, drove past a number of rundown houses and trailers, and found ourselves in downtown Pecos, nothing more than a cross-road. A restaurant named Garcia's looked inviting. We entered and felt like we had traveled back in time. Heavy, dark wooden beams supported adobe walls, and to the right of the doorway at street level was an old bar. Tile steps led to a cluster of tables below. Red, white, and green banners hung from the windows and high beams. Spicy, warm fragrances filled the air. I expected Mexican señoritas in festive folklorico dresses to appear momentarily. Instead, a teenage boy led us to our table. I couldn't wait to have sopapillas, a type of puffy fried bread locals eat with honey. My mouth also watered for enchiladas Christmas style, a dish with both red and green sauces. New Mexican food is like no other.

While we waited for our food, Ric and I looked at old newspaper articles and artifacts displayed in glass cases by the bar. The restaurant was historic, and, as I remembered, most of the Pecos River was in Texas. Its headwaters were a few miles north of us, high in the Sangre de Cristo Mountains. After lunch, we decided to take a drive up the river before continuing on our journey. The road followed a pristine mountain stream flanked by lush green woods and steep canyons. Cabins and fly-fishing resorts appeared around nearly every bend. Who would have thought?

Vowing to return, we headed back and made a quick stop at the Pecos Historical Park to see what it was all about. Again, another surprise. Pecos Pueblo Indians founded a major trade center there, located between the Rio Grande Valley and the plains. They served as middlemen between other Pueblo tribes and Plains Indians. Behind the visitor center were adobe ruins, including the wall of what looked like a church. I couldn't wait to come back when we had more time. Two Indian women sat in the shade outside the restrooms. They were selling jewelry and small woven wall hangings. Jenna and I looked at their wares.

"Look at this, Jenna." I held up a gray weaving with a colorful butterfly in the center. "This would be nice for you to have as your personal symbol. You're starting a journey that could have a huge impact on your life, something like a chrysalis turning into a butterfly. What do you think?"

"It's beautiful," said Jenna.

"Then I'll get it for you. A gift from me to you."

We were expected at Rancho Valmora at 3 p.m., and the school was about an hour away. We passed through Las Vegas without stopping. The small town was located at the edge of the mountains. Dry, hilly land spread east toward the Great Plains. I visualized Apache Indians riding their ponies to trade with the Pecos Pueblo to the west. We could explore later, since Ric and I had reserved a motel for the night.

We drove north from Las Vegas and turned onto a dirt road that followed a brushy creek and passed a few ranches and horse stables. It was a remote spot, and I hoped against hope the setting and school would have a positive influence on her.

We found the school at the end of the road. Entering the grounds we passed a small horse barn. Three friendly dogs ran to greet us. We parked below an old two-story Spanish-style building with a red tile roof and an interior courtyard. Behind us were eight new buildings made to look like haciendas, with thick posts and wide porches. I imagined that was where the kids slept. A huge, new, barn-like structure sat at the far end of the complex.

Later we learned the oldest buildings were

constructed in the early 1900s for a tuberculosis treatment center. The school for teens originally occupied the old buildings. It had expanded in recent years to include the small hacienda dorms and classrooms surrounding a gymnasium in the big barn, an impressive complex.

We found the main office and were greeted by the school's secretary and one of the teachers, Sam. We walked along the wide porch to the office of Terry, the young woman who would be Jenna's counselor and our contact. Terry welcomed us and focused her attention on Jenna.

"Jenna, I bet you're nervous, and not so happy about being here." Jenna nodded slightly but didn't say anything. "I want you to know that this is a very positive place. You will be living with seven other girls. We use something called Positive Peer Culture." She gave a packet to each of us. "What it boils down to is this: you will live, eat, take classes, and play with your group. You will also have therapy together, and once a week you and I will meet one-on-one. We'll call your aunt and uncle when we meet so they can be part of your sessions with me. All the students eat in the dining hall together, but each group has its own table. Sometimes we have whole-school activities, but most of the time you will be with your group. We have found that this is a very successful program. You will also spend considerable time with horses. Equine therapy is a big part of what we do."

Jenna's eyes actually brightened for a moment. She loved riding horses each summer when we visited Elwell Lakes Lodge in the Sierras. Terry picked up on this.

"I love horses too," she said. "My husband and I have a horse ranch just a few miles from here. I often take your group to my ranch to visit the horses and have campfires."

Sam walked us around the campus. First he showed us the old-fashioned ice cream parlor, complete with a counter, stools, and milkshake blenders. Adjoining it was a small recreation room with music and games. We peeked into the empty dining hall next to the office building. Seventy teens were enrolled at the school. There were ten tables, enough for all.

"The students take turns with all the chores here," said Sam. "Each week the work rotates, so at mealtimes some groups are responsible for setting up, serving, and cleaning up while others enjoy being waited upon. We also hold dances here once or twice a month. Let's go see the rest of the school."

As we walked, he showed us landscaping projects around the dorms. Dirt pathways edged with rocks and plants lined the way to the barn. He smiled. "Even though they don't get to spend much time together, there's a lot of competition among the groups. Gardening is one of the electives they all take."

Walking down a slight slope, we passed the first hacienda-style student home. Two boys were sweeping the porch and checked Jenna out as we walked by. She pretended not to notice. We turned toward the second dorm on the lower side of the slope. Its walkway was also lined with rocks, and the adjoining areas were weed free. Planting beds on either side of the building had recently been dug up. A wide porch was welcoming. Sam knocked and walked in.

"Jenna, this is where you'll be living. The girls are in classes right now, so no one is here."

A rustic door opened into a living area with comfortable chairs and a weathered, extra-long picnic table. Two bedrooms were on either side. Each held two sets of bunk beds, four chests of drawers, a closet, and a bathroom. Roomy, but not fancy.

"This will be your bed, Jenna," said Sam. He pointed to one that was made up with a colorful corduroy bedspread. "When we go back to your car, you can get your things and put them away here. I think you'll like your dorm-mates. I know they're looking forward to meeting you." He smiled at Jenna's expressionless face. I was sure he was familiar with all kinds of behaviors from kids first arriving at the school. Few, if any, came of their own will.

At the far end of the living area were an efficiency kitchen on one side and a small bedroom and half bath on the other. "This is where your supervisor sleeps each night. Two adults are assigned to each dorm, one for night and the other for day. Yours are Beth and Laura. They'll be here after school is over. I'm sure you'll like them."

We walked out and headed to the barn-like gymnasium we'd seen earlier. On our right, farther down the slope, were a playing field and a track. Sam said, "We have physical education classes every day and a lot of activities in the afternoons and on the weekends."

Jenna scrunched her nose. Any kind of exertion was way down her list of things she remotely enjoyed. Sam pulled open the gym doors and ushered us inside. "We're really proud of this building. It was finished eighteen months ago and has added a lot to our school. We have a computer lab, a library, and classrooms here in addition to the basketball court and exercise room."

We stood in a foyer that faced glass doors. A beautiful gym was inside. A surrounding hallway opened onto school rooms, currently occupied by students and teachers. The architecture was stunning. It had a western flair with adobe-like walls and big wooden beams but was modern in every sense. I was impressed. The school seemed to be thriving.

When we returned to our rental car with Sam, he pointed to a small barn and corral behind a grove of cottonwood trees. "That's where you'll be working with horses, Jenna," said Sam. He paused. "And this is the time when you say good-bye to your parents."

She gave me a look that I knew meant *they're not my parents*. Ric and I hugged her hard. She responded in her typical slack way: her arms touched my waist but she gave no effort to hug back.

I said to her, "I know this isn't what you want, but I'm confident it's the place you need to be right now. We'll talk to you each week when you're in Terry's office, and I truly hope you can begin to love yourself and work toward living a happy life. I love you."

"Love you too," she said. And turned away.

25

Log Home Search

Quickly approaching was the time to fulfill the pact we made early in our marriage, that Ric would retire as early as he could and we would move to the woods. With points for years worked and age, the magic number was fifty-five. We purchased our Boonville property in January 2000, sixteen months after Jenna came into our lives. We spent several years clearing brush and small trees on our weekend stays and got excited about our building adventure. I had longed for a log home since Ric and I lived in the Sierras during college summers. We subscribed to log home magazines, sketched designs on napkins on date nights, and dreamed. We were on track to retire in 2006 when we were both fifty-five. We made a plan: hire someone to clear about three acres—the only somewhat flat part of our ridgetop land—and build what we called "the barn," a structure with an apartment above and a shop, guest room, bath, laundry, and two-car garage below. We would later rent the living quarters and part of the garage.

By late 2005, after Jenna settled into Rancho Valmora, we were ready to take some concrete steps. One weekend we drove to Sacramento for a log home show at the state fairgrounds. The first thing that struck us when we walked into a huge warehouse was the smell: delicious odors of cedar, pine, and fir wafted in the air. The cavernous space was packed with people and exhibits. Some booths offered handmade log tables, beds, and chairs; others boasted tree-shaped lamps and moose-laden Pendleton blankets. Suppliers displayed metal roofs and custom doors. Child-sized cabins showed various construction styles. Builders from all over the United States and Canada provided advice and brochures.

We walked around like deer in headlights. As we were losing energy, we noticed a large poster listing workshops about design, budgeting, materials, and building your own home. We wandered into a small room where a salesman greeted us and invited us to sit in on a "comprehensive building workshop." We looked at each other and sat down.

We entered as rubes and walked out over-whelmed. Even the speaker's first question had us stumped: "How many of you have made a budget for your project?" Few of the dozen of us raised our hands. He shook his head. "Well, that should be first on your list." Quiet laughter spread across the room. Another memorable tidbit: "Don't worry about what kind of timber to use. They'll all outlast you. Choose what you like."

The main thing we took away was how much we needed to learn. A log home design specialist from Victoria, BC, captivated us because, in addi-tion to clearly being knowledgeable, Cyril Curtois had a charming French accent. We introduced ourselves when the session ended.

"Why don't you attend one of our weekend events where you can learn more and better decide what you want?" he said. "We have one coming up in Phoenix in April."

Ric and I thought Phoenix was an odd loca-tion for a log home workshop, but a spring visit to the desert sounded fun. We put our contact information on a list and told Cyril we might be interested.

Ric's fifty-fifth birthday in December came and went. As it turned out, he wasn't ready to

retire. Change was very hard for him. Most of
the big decisions we made throughout our marriage—buying cars and houses, making travel
plans, looking for and purchasing our property—
were changes I initiated. I was the planner and
pusher while he was the thinker. Frustrated that
he wasn't as anxious as I was to get going on our
big project, I did my best to remain patient.

26

Rancho Valmora

We found Rancho Valmora to be a perfect fit for Jenna. She was exposed to a place, people, and a lifestyle that forced her to think in new ways, to put her own troubles in perspective compared to those of other troubled teens. She liked her roommates, the adult supervisors, and the classes. We maintained communication through our weekly phone visits with her and Terry. It proved to be good for us too.

Every three months or so, we flew from Oakland to Albuquerque, rented a car, and drove two hours over Glorieta Pass into the high plains of eastern New Mexico. After visiting Jenna, we often added a day to our trip, visiting areas of the state we hadn't seen before. We enjoyed learning about Pueblo Indian culture and history, taking back roads through the Sangre de Cristo Mountains and visiting museums in Santa Fe and Albuquerque.

Six months after Jenna went to Rancho Valmora, Annie joined us on one of our visits. It was February 2006. When we arrived, freezing wind attacked our California bodies. We dashed into the administrative building to meet with Terry before visiting Jenna.

"She's doing well," Terry said, "but it's been only six months. She has a lot of hard work to do before she begins to heal. Sometimes I fear she's shining me on, saying what she thinks I want her to say."

"She's an expert at that," I said. "Unfortunately, that's her m.o." I thought for a moment. "I've been wondering what your success rate is with the kids here. Do you keep track of them after they leave?"

"As much as we can, but it's difficult. I wish I could give you better news, but, sadly, I think we have a lasting, positive impact on no more than twenty percent of our students. Most of them have severe trauma and emotional disabilities to overcome, like Jenna does."

"She seems so happy on the phone," I said. "I want to believe she'll get better."

"And she might continue to improve," said Terry. "Time and the amount of effort she puts into her therapy will tell."

As we walked to her dorm, Jenna burst out of the door and rushed toward us, wearing a thin sweater and jeans. She enthusiastically hugged each of us. This is different, I said to myself, grinning.

Jenna smiled and said, "I really want to take you guys on a hike by the river. You'll love it." Her cheeks glowed. She looked like she'd lost weight.

This was not the Jenna I remembered. Ebullient about an outdoor activity and happy to see us? Things had really changed for her. I shivered in the wind. "Aren't you cold?"

"No, I'm used to it."

I asked her where she got the sweater. It wasn't one she brought from home.

"We share all our clothes. This was in the box by the door in my dorm."

We followed her from the parking lot, down past the playing field, and into a mass of tall willows by a creek. She led us along a narrow trail.

"We hike this trail every few days," she said.

Ric and I looked at each other as we walked along. This was amazing. Jenna was bubbly, she had energy, and she seemed to love life. We had never seen her so happy. The high plains wind blew through the ravine and ate into our bones as we made our way through the thicket.

Annie lagged behind. After a bit she called, "Can we go back? It's like the Arctic out here." Jenna seemed disappointed, but she turned around and headed for the school. At the field we ran into a muscled young man with a crew cut.

"You guys, I want you to meet Calvin," said Jenna. "He's my P.E. teacher."

Calvin greeted us and shook our hands. "I don't know if Jenna told you," he said, "but she's one of my best students."

Jenna blushed. I couldn't remember her ever showing embarrassment. The Jenna I knew was unresponsive and sullen.

"Tell them your stats, Jenna."

She hesitated. "Well, I've lost ten pounds and can run the mile without stopping."

"Wow, Jenna," I said. "That's amazing. I'm really proud of you. I've never ever run an entire mile."

Ric and Annie congratulated her as well. We spent another hour with her before having to say our goodbyes. She introduced us to the girls she lived with, shot baskets with us in the gym, and gave us a tour of the horse stables.

"What do you do with the horses, Jenna?" asked Ric.

"Mostly we ride them, but sometimes my group works together in the corral."

"What happens then?" he said.

"It's kind of hard to explain, but we try to get the horse to do what we want him to do without using words. We use our hands and bodies to calm the horse and then get him to move from one side of the corral to the other. It's a teamwork thing. It's hard, but it's pretty fun."

She walked us back to our car and gave each of us bear hugs. I was astonished.

"I hope you can spend an overnight with us the next time we come," I said. "Terry told us if you keep up with your progress, we'll be able to take you to Santa Fe or Albuquerque on our next visit. Would you like that?"

"Yes," she said. "And if it's possible, when we do that, can we go to the Sonic Drive-In and bring a hamburger back for Calvin? He really likes them."

I laughed. "I'm sure we can, Jenna. Think about other things you'd like to do as well."

Driving away, I said to Annie, "You sure were quiet after coming all this way."

"I know. I still feel resentful for all she's put you through, but I'm glad I came. It seems like this place is really working for her."

"I can hardly believe it either," said Ric. "I don't want to get my hopes up after all the times she's sabotaged herself. Let's keep our fingers crossed."

27

Closing In on Retirement

The months wore on. I turned fifty-five in April. That same month we attended the weekend log home event in Phoenix. On Sunday we visited a newly constructed home in a pine forest northeast of the city. It was massive, with hand-carved animals on posts and stairways and wood everywhere—walls, floors, cabinets, furniture. As large as it was, it felt a bit claustrophobic with so much wood. Spectacular, but not for us.

We learned a tremendous amount, narrowed aspects of what we did and didn't want, and returned home serious about planning. Right away we hit a logjam. Over 1,000 log home construction companies were located throughout the States and Canada. Where to start? Digging further, we learned that 90 percent of them used milled logs; each was the same shape so that they were easy to put together. The other 10 percent used handcrafted whole logs. They were custom-cut with chain saws and had a striking, natural look. We found these to be much more to our liking.

Some companies offered "turn-key" homes whereby they hired subcontractors to do all phases of the project, from grading to door locks. That wasn't for us either. Ric wanted to build as much of it as he could, hiring minimal help. My dream was the house and location; his was the project. We began making a list of those companies we might visit west of the Rocky Mountains.

After we returned from Phoenix, Ric still showed no inclination to retire. He would remain fifty-five until the end of the year, so he actually had several months to fulfill the pact. I would need to get my "pusher" role into gear. I decided to set a good example for him by stepping down from my position at Olympic at the end of the school year. When that had no effect, I made plans to take on a part-time job in the fall at Crossroads, a school for pregnant girls and teen moms that was located on the Olympic campus. I enjoyed the staff there and agreed to help students make the transition to college or work after they graduated, very similar to what I did at Olympic but on a smaller scale; Crossroads had two teachers and less than forty students. It was an excellent program, complete with caregivers for infants and toddlers. I enjoyed the work there.

During the summer and fall, I began to tackle preparations for our move to Boonville. Our previous move had been more than twenty years earlier; sorting our possessions wasn't easy. In addition to giving and throwing stuff away, I had to pack for both a year in an apartment and long term for our permanent home. In one way, with Ric at the refinery every day, I took advantage of another difference in our personalities: I liked to make do with what we had while he preferred to save most everything.

One weekend day as I pawed through a large metal construction cart that Brenda, our good friend who was a general contractor, had given us, I came upon a box that hadn't been touched in more than thirty years.

"Here's something we can get rid of," I said to him.

"What is it?"

"A huge box of your college textbooks."

"Oh no. I definitely want to keep those."

"You're kidding." Shaking my head, I sighed

and thanked the gods above he was busy at the refinery instead of overseeing my heavy-handed sorting.

He finally made good on his promise by retiring three weeks before his birthday. He decided to make his retirement a working one, taking on a project at the refinery three days a week, which made the transition easier for him but frustrating for me. He surprised himself (but not me) when weeks into the job he realized he no longer had to join the daily 7:00 a.m. meetings, could go to the gym at 9:00 in the morning instead of 5:00, and could wear Hawaiian shirts to work. He also took woodworking classes two days a week at a nearby adult school. He planned to partner with our friend Wally after we moved, making custom furniture and cabinets.

28

Leaving Valmora

The bone cancer afflicting Jenna's Grandpa Bob worsened. He was her sole remaining grandparent. Ric's mother passed away from her Alzheimer's in 2002 after suffering from the disease for fourteen years. Two years later, six months before Jenna went to Valmora, his dad died from a stroke. Bob's first wife was never in the picture.

Jenna took Bob's illness hard. She received occasional updates from her step-grandmother, Bob's wife, and talked about him frequently. During one session with Terry, she cried out, "Why can't he just die?" Her emotion wasn't surprising, given her close relationship with him, but her outburst was startling. He passed away when she had been at Valmora for a year, and I never heard her talk about him again.

She did, however, continue to improve enough that we could take her off-site occasionally. The first time was a day trip to Las Vegas. We were intrigued with the historic town and looked forward to exploring it. It was famous for being a large stop on the Santa Fe Trail. The year before the railroad reached there, it attracted outlaws and desperados from all over the west, including Doc Holliday, Billy the Kid, Jesse James, and Wyatt Earp. In the town's museum we saw photos of a gallows in the middle of the town square—it had been used countless times. The town gradually settled into a peaceful cattle-grazing community at the eastern foot of the Sangre de Cristo Mountains. Jenna seemed somewhat interested, but we guessed what little enthusiasm she had was due to her being away from the school for the first time.

Once the largest city between Independence, Missouri, and San Francisco, Las Vegas was now a fading community of 15,000. Homes and commercial buildings from the late 1880s dominated downtown. Many storefronts looked like they had been closed for years. We ate lunch at a New Mexican restaurant with a funny, most unusual name: Charlie's Spic & Span Bakery and Café.

It made me wonder if a laundromat hid around the back. It had delicious food; Ric drooled over a chicharón burrito, and as we left we bought two big bags of handmade tortillas, one for Jenna and one for us. Later, we sampled desserts in the Plaza Hotel on the square, a place made famous in the days of the town's lawlessness. We made sure to stop at Sonic so Calvin could get his fix of burgers.

In early December 2006, over a year after she arrived, we arranged to take Jenna to Santa Fe for an overnight. When we picked her up, we had a chance to get to know her roommates better. They were lively and fun. Jenna giggled as she introduced each girl. She seemed happy. Each of the girls had problems serious enough for them to be placed at Valmora, and I couldn't help but wonder about their backgrounds.

In Santa Fe we stayed at our favorite motel, the El Rey. It was a modernized old motor court, moderate in price. Under the motel's sign their slogan was catchy: "If Lucy and Ricky Ricardo had visited Santa Fe, they would have stayed here." Jenna reverted to her passive self. She seemed glad to get away for a night and to see us but showed no excitement about being in Santa Fe. After we settled into our room at the El Rey, I looked through the local brochures we had picked up in the lobby.

"Jenna, is there anything you'd like to do in particular?"

"No, I don't care what we do."

"Hey," I said. "There's a holiday concert in town tonight. Does that sound fun to either of you?"

"Whatever," said Jenna.

"What about you, Ric?"

"I thought we might walk around the plaza to see all the luminarias and Christmas decorations," said Ric.

"Maybe we can do both."

Jenna said, "What's a luminaria?"

Ric explained. "In the Southwest, and especially in New Mexico, luminarias are used to decorate walkways, fences, yards, and roofs. People put sand in paper bags and then light small candles in them. They're also called farolitos. They're beautiful at night and are a special highlight in Santa Fe at Christmas time."

"That sounds nice," said Jenna.

"Let's go to dinner, see the downtown decorations, and then go to the performance. I'll see if we can get tickets." I said.

"The music sounds kind of dumb," said Jenna.

Ric turned to her. "Listen, Aunt Alice really likes music. Unless you can think of something else you'd rather do, I think we should go for her." She didn't object.

The luminarias were breathtaking. We parked near the city plaza and walked several blocks. The little candlelit bags glowed and twinkled in the dark. They were especially stunning around the Saint Francis of Assisi Cathedral and La Fonda Hotel. After our walk, we made our way to the old theater nearby, picked up our tickets from the will call window, and took our seats. I found the program moving; the Santa Fe Symphony played traditional Christmas carols and was accompanied by a city chorus of adults and children. I glanced at Jenna. She looked bored.

Thirty minutes into the program, Jenna leaned over and asked, "Can I go sit in the car?"

I was disappointed but not surprised. "Okay." I gave her the keys to the car and sat back to watch the rest of the show. We were in the middle of a row, and Jenna caused quite a commotion negotiating the narrow seats. Five minutes later, I jolted. I whispered to Ric. "Oh, my God. We gave her the keys to the car! She could take it anywhere." We bothered the same people to get out of the row and rushed to the parking garage. My heart pounded, thoughts raced. But no, there she was, sitting in the car, listening to the radio. Her passivity shined through, this time in a good way.

"We decided to call it a night too," said Ric. I released the breath I had been holding.

Jenna lived at Rancho Valmora for a year and a half. When we first placed her there, we weren't sure if Contra Costa County would pick up the cost or we would have to pay for it. Fortunately, after three months the county and the Martinez school district determined her emotional needs would be best served in a private school. Rancho Valmora was a school they had used before, so she was able to stay there.

A Contra Costa County social worker assigned to Jenna visited her every three months and maintained communication with the school. Early on, she told us she preferred that Jenna be placed nearer our home, but she agreed to leave her where she was as long as she was making good progress. Typical of Jenna's behavior, after first showing real signs of improvement, she continually made a few strides forward and a few steps back. She never got into trouble; rather, she pretty much did nothing but the minimum.

In February 2007 I received a call from Terry, Jenna's therapist at Valmora. "Alice, I think we've done all we can for Jenna. She tries to act like she's improving—she says what she thinks I want her to say—but underneath she isn't willing to do the honest, hard work it will take to make her a healthy person who loves herself as well as others. She's also often a source of trouble in her dorm group. She plays one girl against the other, causing friction."

"I had a feeling this day was coming," I said. "No matter how many wonderful people have tried to help her, she has pushed them all away. You and the staff work incredibly hard for the kids. I'll miss our visits and talks."

The social worker recommended two schools in Petaluma less than an hour's drive from Martinez, a bonus for us. Both were residential and used programs similar to Rancho Valmora's. She had clients at both schools. Ric and I visited each and were most impressed with the Family Life Center (FLC). We met the principal, who showed us their spacious classroom.

"Most of our curriculum is taught via computer, and we're accredited by the state," he told us. He escorted us around the school, told us about their program, and introduced us to Lisa, the on-site therapist. As we drove away, we agreed FLC was worth a try. Rancho Valmora's remote location and program hadn't done much good for her; perhaps this school would spark a light in Jenna. We still had hope.

We flew one last time to New Mexico. True to form, Jenna showed little emotion. Terry and her social worker had prepared her, and she was resigned to the move. Our drive to the

Albuquerque airport was quiet. As we made our way over Glorieta Pass and down into the Rio Grande Valley, I felt a little guilty. As much as I knew Jenna needed to make the move, Ric and I would miss our frequent trips to New Mexico.

"Jenna, are you going to miss Rancho Valmora?" I said.

"Not really."

"What about the P.E. teacher you liked so much? What is his name, Kevin?"

"Calvin."

"It seemed like you might have had a bit of a crush on him."

"He's gay."

Jenna slumped in the seat and stared out the window. She answered our questions with as few words as possible. She pretended to sleep on the airplane.

After we landed at SFO, we took Jenna directly to Petaluma as the staff had recommended. The Family Life Center occupied a property on the town's outskirts. Behind two old ranch homes were a newly constructed classroom, a modular office building, and a basketball court. A rail fence separated the school from a flock of sheep. The yard was beautifully landscaped; gardening was a big part of the students' responsibilities. Up to twelve girls were housed in the ranch houses. A group home two miles away was available to an additional six girls who excelled in the program. Both community college classes and in-town, part-time jobs were options for students who met the high standards of the school in behavior and academics. While she never reached those levels, Jenna did well at FLC during the eighteen months she was there. I made weekly trips for therapy sessions with Lisa and Jenna. Ric came with me when he could.

Lisa developed an easy rapport with Jenna. They often made jewelry together while they talked. Lisa seemed to be making inroads. One day when I arrived, Jenna ran to meet me, hugged me, and said, "Hi, Mom." This was a first; we had always been Uncle Ric and Aunt Alice. Even though the words sounded a little forced, it was progress. Her hug was another surprise. Normally she was limp as a rag. I remembered when she had reacted similarly at Rancho Valmora, then fell back. *Don't get your hopes up.*

I was pleased with the online, self-paced curriculum. Students were challenged with the same standards as those in public schools. In addition, FLC stressed life skills; high school graduates of FLC were equipped with resources to assist them as they transitioned to independent living.

29

Fun Times

We readied our property for construction by hiring people to put in a well, a septic system, and electricity. None of the work was easy, and all of it was expensive. Ric's dad had loaned us money to purchase the property and do the site work. We planned to get a construction loan for the barn and use our twenty-year equity from the sale of our Sage Drive house to fund the log home.

After doing a lot of research about western log home companies, in early fall 2007, six months after Jenna enrolled at the Family Life Center, we took a two-week road trip in a huge loop through northern California, Oregon, Washington, British

Columbia, Montana, and Idaho. We toured a
dozen businesses ranging from a one-man opera-
tion in a muddy clearing to a huge company near
Boise, Idaho, where CAD designers sat in cubicles
and Hispanic workers built each home under a
near–football field sized roof. Our most northerly
stop was 100 Mile House, a small community in
central BC that billed itself as the Handcrafted
Log Home Building Capital of North America.
The town's September weather surprised me; it
was two feet deep in snow. Slogging around the
slushy yards reminded us why we lived in California. Stunning country but a harsh climate. I
still use the inexpensive knit gloves I bought to
brave the cold temperatures there.

The company we liked best was a small
outfit seventy miles east of Vancouver and, as
it happened, not far from our French-Canadian
designer acquaintance, Cyril Curtois. The owner
of Cascade Handcrafted Log Homes, his partner,
and their small staff built two to three homes in
their yard each year, from two-room weekend
cabins to grand lodges. They were low key, open,
and friendly.

When we returned from our trip, construction began on the barn. A local designer made
blueprints from Ric's sketches. John, the builder
we hired, had a crew of two. Ric planned to work

alongside them when he could. All we needed now was a laborer.

The Mendocino County Fair and Apple Show is always held the third weekend in September at the fairgrounds in Boonville. It's a classic county fair—it has all the 4-H animals; quilt, jam, and vegetable displays; carnival rides; rodeos; and calorie-laden fair food—but it's on a small scale in accordance with the size of the county. It's a very big deal for residents. Ric and I were wandering around when we ran into Wally and Sue.

"Hey, Wally," Ric said. "Do you happen to know anyone who would be a good laborer for our barn project?"

"As a matter of fact, I do. Jose Luis has been doing work for me and could use a steady job. He's getting married soon." He glanced around. "And what do you know? There he is."

Wally walked us over to a young couple and introduced us. Jose was a handsome, friendly young man who had his arm around his girlfriend. A minute later he agreed to start work on Monday, two days away. Life in a small town was all I hoped it would be.

Ric, finally fully retired, stayed in our little leaky trailer and came home most weekends. I was frustrated that he was there and I was stuck at home with weekly commitments to Jenna as well as to our dog, who had cancer and needed regular chemo treatments. The months crawled for me, but Ric was in his element, loving every minute. I came up to the property often, staying in our little trailer, but there really wasn't much for me to do. The grunt work Jose Luis did was not appealing to me, and I had few construction skills. I just wanted it done.

We worked with Cyril Curtois on the design of our future home over the phone and via computer. Ric sent him detailed sketches. In his wonderful French accent, Cyril responded, "Reek, your design is detailed and complete. It eez nearly perfect. There are just a few changes I would recommend."

Ric laughed. "Do you mean you'd like it to be less engineered?"

"Exactly."

Cyril had an interesting trademark: towers. When he sent us back a draft of the design, I was taken aback. Taking in all our desires, the house was enormous: the dining room was within an eight-foot-diameter octagon twelve feet high; above the main floor was a catwalk connecting two rooms of extra space; and the lower floor had two guest rooms, a bathroom, a family room, and a huge storage area. The garage would be a separate building. We accepted his plan, but

I hoped to talk Ric into scaling it down before we built it. It was a dream house for a family of eight, not two.

Ric and I treated our family to a short cruise to Cabo San Lucas for the Thanksgiving holiday. Lisa and other school officials agreed that some family time would be very good for Jenna; a cruise, where she would be unable to stray, also seemed a good choice. She acted excited when we told her about the vacation. Sara and Annie weren't thrilled with our including her but agreed it might be good for Jenna. We invited my cousin Milly and her husband, Marvin, who lived near San Diego where the cruise began and ended. While I never thought I'd enjoy being stuck on a huge ship filled with hordes of people eager to stuff their faces, I knew our girls would love it, and having fun-loving Milly along would make it even better.

The seven of us embarked on the enormous Carnival Princess the day after Thanksgiving. Just as I'd feared, I felt like a cow in a herd, being shoved from corral to chute. We waited in line to board and then were directed to elevators that took us to our rooms on a lower deck of the monster ship. The girls were giddy with excitement while I tried to mask my impatience. I noticed Jenna checking out other kids in line. She knew there was a special club for teens, and we told her if she maintained good behavior and a positive attitude, she could spend time there.

Once we found our minuscule rooms and unpacked, we explored. Together we checked out the gaudy shops, restaurants, bars, and pool areas. I found out right away the inexpensive cruise rates were a lure; only the basics were covered. Even soft drinks were exorbitant. Camping in a tent was much more my style, but I kept my mouth closed, not wanting to spoil it for the others.

We found the teen club off the pool deck. Jenna entered and came back in a minute, disappointed. "It looks more like it's for teeny boppers," she said.

"Make the best of it, Jenna," I said. "I bet it will pick up in the evening. The pool area looks fun. There's a stage for outdoor entertainment." She rolled her eyes but didn't complain. I hoped she was thinking how lucky she was to be on the cruise at all, but I doubted it registered.

Even though it was November, I assumed the temperature south of San Diego would be warm. Wrong. It was chilly and windy the entire way. Jenna became enamored with a rock group that played by the pool, and it was all I could do to convince family members to hang out with her there; we had promised the FLC staff we'd never let her out of our sight. I won't forget wonderful

Marvin, wrapped in a blanket, sitting in a lounge chair next to Jenna for much of one afternoon. He is a very patient man.

We stopped in Ensenada on the way to Cabo San Lucas. There we had two excursion choices: riding ATVs or wine tasting. Annie, Milly, and I wanted to try the quads but Jenna didn't. That left her with Ric, Sara, and Marvin on a bus to "one of Mexico's finest wineries." We off-roaders had a good time, although it wasn't at all on the wild side. It took the thirty of us more than a half hour to be educated on the safety and mechanics of the vehicles. The staff then gave us keepsake kerchiefs, which I found were useful for filtering the dust of the riders directly in front of us as we rode up and down the dry rows of a vineyard. Fortunately, Milly kept Annie and me in stitches as she yahooed and took pictures of us over her shoulder on the fly. Later, when we compared notes, we found we had the better of the two experiences; not only was the wine lousy, but Jenna did her best to draw any fun there might have been out of the afternoon, sulking and moping.

We all looked forward to snorkeling in Cabo San Lucas, even Jenna. We lounged on the deck of a large catamaran as it motored to a nearby cove. Sara and Annie posed like goons in their lime-green masks and snorkels. When we got to the cove and donned our gear, all of us except

Jenna jumped in. I came up for a breath and looked back. "Jenna, come on in, it's great," I said.

"I'm scared. I've never done this before."

"You'll do fine. You're a good swimmer and the water is clear." She slowly slid into the water and lowered the mask. Up she popped.

"Ewww. There are so many fish."

"That's the point, Jenna," I said. I sucked in a breath and dove, comfortable given my years of scuba diving. Under the surface it was hysterical: above me was a mass of iridescent green duck feet flapping under Day-Glo orange life vests, cruisers' faces peering into the water. The poor fish didn't have a chance.

When I came up again, I saw Jenna climbing back aboard the sailboat. Another chance to distance herself from a good time. During the entire cruise, the only time I saw her truly enjoy herself was in the photography studio. We all donned crazy Mexican costumes with props of maracas, serapes, and guitars. The employees had a terrific shtick; we came home with seventy-five dollars' worth of forgettable photos.

30

Graduation

The last two months of Jenna's stay at Family Life Center were charged with success. She burned through the school curriculum, and her therapy sessions went well. She was excited at the chance to come home and get on with her life. She met all qualifications by mid-April, which meant she would graduate early.

Ric, Sara, Annie, and I joined her on her special day. Since the students worked at their own pace, most often each was given her own ceremony. Set up with chairs, the living room of the main house displayed pieces of Jenna's artwork and written assignments. The place was packed

with all the staff and students. As the graduation march played on a cassette recorder, Jenna
walked to the front of the room in black cap and
gown, radiant. She stood tall, her dark brown,
shoulder-length hair shining. One by one, staff
members and her peers came forward and spoke
about how proud they were of her achievements
and progress during the eighteen months she was
at FLC. Then it was Jenna's turn.

"When I arrived," she said, "this was the last
place I wanted to be. I was much closer to home,
yet I might as well have still been several states
away. I couldn't contact my friends and I couldn't
leave. I was angry and felt stuck. The only time
I was able to get away was for a family vacation,
and it was almost like jail, I had so little freedom.
Here I am a year and a half later, excited to get
on with my life. What happened in between to
make me change?" She paused. "All of you in
this room had a part in helping me become the
person I am today."

She took time to mention each staff member and student, either individually or in small
groups, thanking them for what they had done
for her. Then she looked at us. I had tears in my
eyes and so did she. Who would have ever thought
Jenna would be standing in front of us, a beautiful
young woman, speaking from her heart and so
happy with herself?

"Mom, Dad, I have dragged you through hell." The room burst with laughter. "You have put up with me for almost ten years, and you have never given up on me. There were times I hated you, furious that you kept me away from my mother and my life with her. Deep down I knew you were right, but I never admitted it, most times even to myself. I was convinced the world was against me. I had no hope. It took a long, long time, but finally, and especially with Lisa's help, I began to believe in myself. I hope I can make you proud of me from this day on." Ric held my hand tightly as I crushed a moist wad of tissues.

"Sara and Annie, I have been the worst cousin and sister you could have possibly imagined. I know you felt Mom and Dad gave me more attention and love than I deserved. I hope you will find it in your hearts to give me another chance to be part of our family." Both girls wiped their eyes.

Jenna picked up a thick binder and held it in front of her. "FLC has prepared me with resources and ways I can help myself become independent. I worked hard to complete all the assignments. I feel ready to get a job and start taking classes at Diablo Valley College. I don't know what I want to study, but I do want to transfer to a four-year college and make something of myself." By this time, mascara ran down her cheeks. She glowed with confidence.

The school principal asked if anyone else wanted to speak. I raised my hand and stood up.

"When Jenna was in third grade, shortly after she moved in with us, she went with me to the lumberyard. Ric needed some materials for a backyard project and I offered to go. Halfway home she said, 'I thought you're supposed to put a red flag on the end of anything hanging out of a pickup truck.'

"Always eager for teachable moments, I said, 'You're right, Jenna, but only if it hangs out more than three feet. These two-by-fours are ten feet long, and the bed of Uncle Ric's truck is eight feet long. How many feet are hanging over?'

"I knew she could do this simple problem, but she remained silent. I waited and finally said, 'Come on, Jenna. I know you can do this. Think about it. The truck bed is eight feet long and the wood is ten feet long. What's the difference in length?'

"Silence. By this time I began to think she wasn't answering on purpose, just to make me mad. I pulled over to the side of the road and stopped. I was terribly frustrated with the way she always seemed to sabotage herself. 'Jenna,' I said, 'I am not going to let you fail.'

"She looked me in the eye and said, 'I'll fail if

I want to.' Stunned, I stared at the steering wheel. I thought for a moment while she continued to glare at me. 'You know, Jenna,' I said, 'you're right. But I'm going to do everything I can to keep you from failing.' I pulled away from the curb, she turned forward, and we drove home in silence."

I looked at Jenna. "Even though you did your best to fail time and time again, look at you now. I am amazed at how far you've come. I am very, very proud of you."

Inside, I was conflicted. Certainly I was proud of Jenna for completing her program, but she excelled at self-sabotage. There had never been a time when she maintained any kind of success. Would she do it this time? Was she truly a different person, ready to work hard and accomplish goals? If I had to bet, I would say no, but there was always hope. That's the feeling I had; I was hopeful.

31

Double Disaster

When even walking became debilitating, in June 2007, I had my knee replaced. I had severely injured it skiing when I was twenty-seven, and after two arthroscopies in my thirties, my orthopedic surgeon told me there was nothing more he could do. By the time I was fifty, he said, "Most likely aches in your knee will change with the weather, and by fifty-five you'll need a new knee."

As much as I loved sports and hiking, over the years I had to eliminate activities one by one until all I could do was walk. I checked in with the doctor when the pain became severe. He was near perfect with his prediction; I had the surgery two months after my fifty-sixth birthday. Jenna was a junior at the Family Life Center at this time.

Ric had retired from the refinery six months earlier and worked part time as a contract employee there. He was an excellent nurse. After the surgery I spent several weeks in Annie's old bedroom on the main floor of our house with easy access to the bathroom and kitchen. We put a small TV at the foot of the bed. Later Ric joked about the danger he had put in front of me. He said I spent those days watching the Travel Channel on Vicodin with my Visa card at the ready. In actuality I did book two trips: one, the Carnival Cruise to Cabo, and the other, a grand adventure.

As I watched an enchanting show about rafting through the Grand Canyon, an idea began to form. For over thirty years my dad had encouraged us to do that rafting trip. He went with friends in 1974 and raved about it. In my sickbed I decided to honor Dad by booking a trip with as many family members and friends as I could. He was ninety-six at the time, and I knew he'd get a kick out of my plan. Twelve people, including my two brothers and three of my cousins, signed on. I booked the trip for early May, a year after my surgery.

We didn't invite Sara and Annie. It was very expensive, and since they preferred shopping to the outdoors, I knew they would neither appreciate nor enjoy it.

I spent many months looking forward to and preparing for our adventure. What I hadn't foreseen was Jenna's early graduation in April. As soon as I realized the conflict, I racked my brain for a solution. Brenda became our savior. She knew Jenna well and was used to dealing with difficult situations and people. Single, and flexible with her working time, she was the perfect person to fill in for us. It would be a relief to have her stay in our house and leave Jenna in her hands.

After her graduation Jenna was happy to be back in Martinez and began to reconnect with friends she had left three years before. She expressed interest in attending the Summer Institute at Diablo Valley College, a program for at-risk teens making the transition from high school to college. Using skills she learned at the Family Life Center, she began to search for a job. We talked about her getting a learner's permit so she could obtain a driver's license.

I was excited about Jenna's future and our upcoming retirement. In September, less than five months away, Jenna would turn eighteen. I couldn't wait to start my dream life in the woods. On an emotional high, a few days after Jenna's graduation I thought it would be a good time to quit taking Depakote, the medication I took for bipolar syndrome. I had used it effectively for more than five years, but I really wanted to wean myself off the drug. Feeling stable and strong, I made an appointment with my psychiatrist.

Although I hadn't seen him since he first prescribed the medication, he still made me feel uncomfortable with his superficial manner and sleazy looks. Within minutes he agreed that perhaps my struggles had been triggered by our difficulties in raising Jenna. "Perhaps this was all situational," he said. He suggested I start by cutting the dosage of Depakote in half.

Within three days I began to spiral down. We had already invited our friends, the Finn family, to spend the weekend visiting us in Boonville. Jenna, newly home, joined us with Sara. Fearful of my declining mental state, I reluctantly went along.

The first day we went wine tasting at Roederer Estate Vineyards near Boonville. The Finns' three kids and Jenna found a comfortable couch adjacent to the tasting bar. I joined them there, silent. I can't remember how I got through the rest of the day, but by morning I couldn't get out of bed.

The first phase of our barn project was nearly complete, though we didn't plan to move until we sold our house in Martinez. We had brought a bed from home that was much more comfortable than the little trailer's thin mattress. Sara slept in the guest room downstairs on an air mattress, and Jenna set herself up on the living room couch outside our bedroom.

The Finns stayed at Wally and Sue's guest house fifteen minutes away. My depression had sunk so low that when they arrived the following morning for a sourdough pancake breakfast, I knew I couldn't face them, let alone organize and prepare a meal. We hadn't installed a stove yet, so Sara and Ric cooked in the trailer. Below me I could hear the group laughing and talking while my cheek felt glued to the bed, my head dead weight. At one point I heard a slight noise and opened one eye. Jenna was staring at me from the living room. I slowly closed my eye, and a bit later I heard her walk downstairs.

I began to have suicidal thoughts again, exactly like at Christmastime years earlier. Pain and helplessness seemed insurmountable. Fringes of my brain understood something important, however: suicide leaves a deadly aftermath for loved ones. After living through young Michael's suicide and the trauma it caused his family and Annie, I tried to think of a way to die as if it were an accident. I dwelt on slamming my Miata into a freeway abutment, out of control.

It didn't occur to me that Ric was fully aware of the extent of my depression. Later he came in, sat next to me and said, "There's an elephant in the room, isn't there?"

I nodded. "I'm desperately depressed again."

"You didn't talk about your feelings, but I could tell you were beginning to descend into that abyss. First thing," he said, "let's put you back on your old dosage. We know it's going to take a while, but we'll do this together." I couldn't lift my head, but nodded. He was able to get through to me and made me promise not to hurt myself. I didn't tell him of my tentative plan.

As I listened, I said, "I don't know why I tried to get off Depakote at all. I'm never going to get off these drugs, Ric. It's not worth it."

"Let's deal with that when you feel better. I'll call the mental health clinic as soon as we get home. Think about last time. It took a few weeks, but you gradually became your old self."

I remembered the deep well I had fallen into before and how, despite its seeming to take forever, I eventually crawled out of it. "I don't know if I can go through that again. It was a nightmare."

"I'll be right by your side," said Ric.

I recalled the long days at home when I felt petrified to see anyone, played innumerable games of solitaire and gin rummy, and stared at the floor of my office when I went back to work. The inability to focus, the dark cloud that followed me wherever I went, the hopelessness and worthlessness, the heaviness of it all. I remembered how dependent I was on Ric and how he kept our home and me together. I squeezed his hand. My rock.

I dragged myself through the next days. After one week at home, Jenna's newfound exuberance for life disappeared. Old habits took its place: lies, sullenness, and deception. I suppose having to deal with her actually helped me move forward. One day she asked to walk the half mile to the shopping center where we bought groceries so she could get some exercise. Had I been thinking clearly, I likely would have refused. After an hour I began to worry. I got into the car and drove the route she would have taken, scanning every block. I found her in the corner Burger King, the first place I looked. She sat in a booth with a thuggish-looking guy in a muscle shirt who looked to be in his thirties. She recoiled when I called her name but didn't hesitate when I told her to come with me.

On the drive home I asked her who the man was. Her answer was vague: "He's a friend I met through Ieshia," she said. "He just happened to be at Burger King." I wanted to believe her, but my instinct and experience told me she had set up the encounter.

She had been spending a lot of time on the computer in the loft office outside our bedroom.

Whenever I climbed the stairs and glanced at her, I had the impression she clicked from one window to another, hiding what she was doing. The more I distrusted her, the more she acted like the old Jenna.

Although my mental state was frail, I was determined to go on our Grand Canyon trip. We anticipated problems while we were gone on our two-week adventure, so we first made a behavior contract with Jenna. She was to do household chores, look for work, and make sure Brenda knew of her whereabouts and activities. This was an opportunity for her to show us she had changed. While it was risky to leave her home alone while Brenda was working, our friend was our best choice. After all, Brenda would handle any situation the same way we would.

We crossed our fingers and left by car for Lees Ferry, Arizona. The two-day drive was uneventful, and when we talked to Brenda before we took off on the rafts, all was good at home. After the call we looked at each other and crossed our fingers at the same time.

During the first few days, Brenda felt the same uneasiness we had. Jenna stayed in her room most of the time or sat in front of the computer or TV, interacting with Brenda only when she had to. In one sense you couldn't blame her. I was sure that after living in boarding schools for three years and graduating from high school, she felt like a prisoner. On the other hand, she had a lot to prove to us. We had always been clear with her: either she acted like she wanted to be part of our family or she would have to find another place to live when she turned eighteen. Over the years she had continually pushed us away, testing our love and commitment. Now, with her eighteenth birthday four months away, there was little time for her to show us she was trustworthy, a major value in our family.

One of Jenna's chores was to feed our dog, Buddy. Early one morning, when Brenda was taking a shower, Jenna knocked on the loft bathroom door and called out, "I've already fed Buddy, so you don't need to worry." It was out of character for Jenna to be up early—alarm bells rang in Brenda's head. Buddy's dish was in our family room on the lower floor, a walk-out basement. Jenna's bedroom was on the main floor below ours. After dressing, Brenda went down the basement stairs to the family room. She smelled alcohol. Now the bells clanged. As she rounded the corner at the bottom of the stairs, a three-alarm fire greeted her: several young men were passed out on the couches and floor. The room was littered with bottles and fast-food containers.

Brenda was enraged, but she had an important business meeting early that morning. Rather than getting into it with Jenna then, she put a note on her door: *I will be back at 8:30 a.m. Get those boys out of here, clean the house, and be ready to talk to me when I return.*

Two hours later, as Brenda berated her, Jenna assumed her classic passive stance: she sat meekly with no visible reaction. Later Brenda told us she had tied Jenna to her with an invisible tether until we returned. Jenna went with her to work, sat in on meetings, and slept next to her bed on the floor. It amazed me that Jenna didn't take off, but that was her nature: to withdraw and show no emotion when under stress.

In the meantime, I was doing my best to have a good time with our friends and family. The first evening, we all sat in a circle in our camp chairs, enjoying drinks and snacks and sharing stories from the day. Our friend Nancy sat next to me. Leaning over, she said, "You're awfully quiet."

I shrugged my shoulders. "I just don't feel like talking. I'm pooped." I tried very hard to be a part of the group, but excited wasn't a word I would use to describe my feelings while the rest were having the time of their lives.

Arizona River Runners was a quality outfit and gave us a memorable adventure: raging rapids, incredible scenery, delicious meals, and intriguing stories about the history and geology of the canyon. It would have been thrilling without the weight of depression on my shoulders. A helicopter picked us up after six days, a spectacular end to our adventure. While new guests flew down and floated the rest of the river, we 'coptered straight up between the massive canyon walls and landed at a large dude ranch. The exhilarating flight was actually my favorite part of the trip, maybe because I was feeling a little better each day. A hot shower had never been more rejuvenating. A small plane flew us back to Lees Ferry.

Brenda didn't contact us at the motel there. She knew our schedule, so we figured all was good. On her end, delivering the news by phone would serve no purpose other than to ruin the rest of our vacation.

As we had planned, we added two extra days to the raft trip to visit Canyonlands and Arches national parks. I did my best to enjoy them. We hiked through vast deserts with colorful canyons, steep cliffs, wondrous rock formations, and expansive vistas. It couldn't have been a better place to work through my slump. When I heard myself whistling as I walked down Park Avenue, a broad, winding red rock trail lined with monoliths reaching for the sky, I knew I had rounded a bend on the road to recovery. Facing a disaster when we returned home was the last thing on my mind.

32

Three Balls Drop

Ric and I left Moab, Utah, early in the morning and drove as far as Reno. We decided to take Highway 50 from Utah, not only to avoid boring I-80 but to revisit the route; thirty years earlier we had driven that road coming home from our honeymoon in British Columbia. It was still monotonous, as it traversed 700 miles of uninhabited desert, but at least it wasn't the multi-lane Interstate with repetitive Denny's and mega truck stops.

"Let's not tempt fate like we did last time, okay?" I said. We laughed, recalling nearly running out of gas on a long stretch between Ely and Fallon, Nevada. We'd had no idea there were no gas stations. When we finally made it to Fallon, the tank took more than it was supposed to hold.

I called Brenda from the motel in Reno to let her know our plan.

"I have some bad news," said Brenda.

My stomach rolled. "Something happened with Jenna, right?"

"How did you guess?"

"Lay it on me. I want to know the worst of it before I get home."

Brenda described the nightmare of Jenna's behavior, sparing no details.

"Oh my God," I said. "How are *you*?"

"I'm fine," Brenda said. "You know me. It takes a lot to knock me down. She's been meek as a kitten since the party. She's made the entire time utterly joyless, but that's okay. I'm thrilled you're coming home, however. I need to focus on work and quit worrying about her."

After I hung up and told Ric what Jenna had done, I didn't hesitate to tell him my feelings. "I'm done. Jenna knew exactly what was at stake, and she blew it. I'm not going to live having to anticipate what she'll do next. I just knew her graduation high would disappear quickly. Another opportunity to sabotage herself. I know she's not yet eighteen, but I'm going to figure out a way to have her live somewhere else."

"Are you sure?" said Ric. "You don't want to see this through until September?"

"I'm not going to do it. She has pushed us away for too long without ever giving us an ounce of love or caring. I'm done. If you have a better idea, I'm happy to hear it."

Jenna was in her room when we got home. I went in to see her while Ric walked Brenda to her car. I said to Jenna, "On the phone last night Brenda told us what you did while we were gone. I want you to meet us in the kitchen in a half hour after we unload the car. We'll talk then."

She said nothing and gave me her familiar blank stare. I closed the door, feeling more certain of our decision.

The three of us sat at the kitchen table. "Here's what's going to happen," I said. "You're going to find a new place to live. We're not going to put up with your disrespect. For the time being we'll support you financially and will help you with your needs, but you can't live under our roof."

Her eyes widened.

"It's almost impossible to believe that less than a month ago you were on top of the world, ready to be part of our family and get on with a productive life, but now here we are, right back where we were three years ago when you stole Ric's truck and we sent you to boarding school.

You have had countless people try to help you. You have continually pushed away everyone who has cared about you. Uncle Ric and I are done. You're on your own."

"Your Aunt Alice has spent the past ten years giving you her all," said Ric. "The rest of us have done what we could, but she's the one who basically put her life on hold to give you a chance to have a happy life. Do you have anything at all to say to us?"

"How long do I have?" said Jenna.

Inside, I reeled. Not an apology, no pleading for another chance, nothing. I shouldn't have been surprised, but after all these years, her soulless nature still baffled me. I took a deep breath before I answered.

"You have a week to research possibilities. If you haven't found anything by then, we'll get involved and find something for you."

Two days later, Jenna found an apartment to share a few miles away. Her time at the Family Life Center had not been wasted, given the independent living skills she learned there. Maybe this would prove to be a very good thing for all of us. No matter how ridiculous it might have been, I was hopeful, again.

I drove her to meet her potential roommate. Samantha was an attractive twenty-four-year-old who had a good job but needed someone to share costs. The girls seemed to like each other. The apartment complex was decent, nothing fancy. It was located close to Highway 4, where Jenna would have easy access to public transportation. I told Samantha we were responsible for Jenna, given her age. We made arrangements to pay rent and utilities and set up a time to move her things.

We kept in contact with Jenna by phone, and things seemed to be going well. She said she had a friend who would drive her to the orientation for the Summer Institute at Diablo Valley College, and she was looking for work. The same friend did some catering and might be able to get jobs for her with his employer.

The first ball dropped when I called the supervisor of the Summer Institute, a woman I had worked closely with when I worked at Olympic High School.

"Hi, Debra. Jenna told me she went to the orientation on Saturday."

"No," said Debra. "I specifically looked for her. She didn't sign in, and she wasn't there."

"Damn," I said. "Here we go again."

Why was I not surprised when Jenna later insisted she had been there? There was no arguing with her. She would never back down even though she knew I knew she was lying.

The next two months were relatively quiet. We paid her rent, gave her living expenses, and talked with her occasionally. Then the second ball dropped. In early August, Samantha called to tell us Jenna had to move out.

"What happened?"

"She's been hanging around with a drug dealer who lives upstairs. I can't afford to get into trouble because of her."

Jenna's next stop was with the family who had befriended her in third grade, the Nelsons. They had always felt sorry for her and included her in many activities. Their daughter Bridget was set to start Diablo Valley College in the fall. I told them their generous assistance might very well blow up in their faces, but they were willing to take the chance. They gave her until October to enroll in school or find a job—too much time, to my mind.

In mid-September I received a phone call.

"Hi. I'm calling from a cell phone my daughter found in Rankin Park," said a woman. "There is a contact listed 'home' and I thought you might know whose phone this is."

"I'll be right there," I said. Sure enough, it was Jenna's. I drove to the Nelsons' house and knocked. It was two in the afternoon. Jenna answered in a bathrobe. Her hair was a mess.

"Here's your phone," I said. "Someone found it at the park."

She took it from me and said, "Thanks." I turned and walked away as she shut the door.

The third ball dropped. By October Jenna had neither found a job nor enrolled in school, and the Nelsons asked her to leave. She responded by stealing jewelry and credit cards from their home. Then she disappeared.

Given her resourcefulness, I knew she would survive. Ric and I got on with our new lives, preparing to sell our house and move to Boonville.

33

Hopeful, Again

After Jenna left our house in summer 2008, Brenda asked us if we'd like a roommate. Her latest construction project was a large apartment complex in Emeryville, and the project manager she hired lived over two hours away in Merced. Rather than put him up in a motel during the week, she thought the arrangement would be a good deal for all of us: Neil would have a comfortable place to stay, and the rent we received from Brenda would help offset expenses to maintain our two homes in Martinez and Boonville.

When Brenda brought Neil to meet us, I thought I was meeting John Muir reincarnate. Gangly, with a bushy beard, he looked very much like the famous naturalist who lived in Martinez in the late 1800s when he wasn't traipsing off to the Sierras or Alaska. Amazingly, it turned out Neil was a long-distant cousin of Muir. Ric and I liked him right away. He was easygoing and chuckled deeply when he laughed. In no time we were eating dinner together the four nights a week when he stayed at our house, and we enjoyed sharing stories.

While he had never met Jenna, Neil experienced her in a way that left him with no doubt about the sordid tales we told him. In mid-September, when Jenna was living with the Nelsons, I called to tell her we would be in Boonville for a few days. With no phone or cell service at our property, I always made sure she knew whom to call in our absence if there was an emergency.

I doubted it was for spite—that wasn't Jenna's nature—rather, she probably saw a golden opportunity and took it. When Neil arrived Monday evening, he found empty liquor bottles, dirty diapers, cigarette butts, pizza cartons: overall, a disgusting mess. He cleaned it up before we returned the following day. We felt terrible when he told us what had happened, but he shrugged it off. "I raised two teenage girls too," he said.

Neil was right; almost all the trouble Jenna got into was not unusual for kids and teenagers.

Our own daughters had a few parties when we were gone, and I myself had done the same. But most kids feel guilt and remorse when they are caught. It was the number of times she did it and her lack of any reaction when we confronted her that wore us down. We were tired of dealing with her lack of respect.

I called Nancy Nelson—I was sure it was Jenna who had instigated the party. As it turned out, Nancy already knew about it. Jenna had convinced Bridget, Nancy's daughter, to come with her. Bridget got scared when she saw the tough-looking guys who were there and returned home. When Nancy confronted Jenna, her response was her usual deadpan gaze.

By fall 2008 we were ready to sell our Sage Drive house. Resembling a Tahoe cabin, it would only appeal to buyers who appreciated its unique design. It was terribly unfortunate that at the very same time, our country was spiraling into a deep recession. We had no takers. One couple was interested, but they weren't in a position to buy it. We waited and maintained both places.

Seven months after the Nelsons asked Jenna to leave, a good friend called. "You'll never guess who I saw at the homeless shelter when I was serving lunch today. Jenna was there with a young man, looking ready to pop with a baby."

At dinner that night, with a twinkle in his

eye, Neil said, "Dollars to doughnuts you'll be taking care of that baby before long."

"You don't know me very well, Neil," I laughed. "When I said I was done, I meant it. I rarely go back on my word. Jenna knows that too. Want to make a bet?"

"Okay," said Neil. "How about a hundred dollars says you'll be involved with that baby within six months?"

I reached across the table and shook his hand. "Be prepared to open your wallet."

Neil moved back to his home in the Central Valley, and over time our friendship languished. I have yet to collect that money from him.

I was disappointed that Jenna was pregnant, but it didn't surprise me. I assumed after the Nelsons kicked her out she would drift to the first warm bed she found. I thought about calling her—we still paid for her cell phone—but decided against it. She knew where we were if she wanted to talk to us.

Finally, by June, we were ready to move. The one couple who had an interest in the house agreed to sign an eighteen-month lease, intending to purchase at the end of it. We put our log home on hold; we couldn't afford to build without the equity we had earned over more than twenty years of ownership.

Shortly before we cleaned out the house, the

phone rang. "Hi, Aunt Alice," said a familiar voice on the phone.

"Jenna, how are you?"

"I'm actually very good." My heart skipped. "I have a beautiful little boy named Jason. His dad and I got family housing from Social Services, and Brian has a job as a nighttime security guard." I could hear her smile on the other end of the phone.

"That's fantastic, Jenna. I'm happy you have been able to take care of yourself."

"I wonder if I can ask a favor of you," said Jenna. "I need a copy of my birth certificate, and I think there's one at the house."

"Of course. I know exactly where it is. Can Uncle Ric and I bring it to you? I'd love to see your baby and meet your boyfriend."

Four days later, Ric and I pulled into the driveway of a small apartment complex in Pittsburg. The buildings were well kept and looked new. Jenna and her little family stood next to a black pickup truck in the parking lot and she waved. I got out, hugged her, and gave her a baby gift along with her birth certificate. She actually squeezed me back, ever so slightly. She introduced us to Brian and let me hold Jason, a darling baby with black curly hair and dark-as-night eyes. Brian had graduated from Alhambra High School in Martinez and seemed like a nice young man.

A week later I called Jenna. "You know, we still have money your grandfathers left for you in our care. I'm sure you can use some extra beyond what you receive from the county and Brian's income. If you're willing to let us help you manage your money, we'll set up an account for you at the credit union and deposit money monthly."

"That would be awesome," said Jenna.

Jenna's grandfathers had each left us $10,000 for her. We hadn't used any of the money yet, and with a baby to care for, we were hopeful, once again, that she might turn herself around. She did what we asked. She had a debit card linked to her credit union account. We received monthly statements listing her expenditures. We weren't impressed with some of her purchases, such as fast food and pedicures, but we tried to remain positive.

In July 2009 Jenna called to ask if we would pay for a medical assistant program through the Pittsburg Adult School.

"Jenna," I said, "that's wonderful. The health career field is wide open, and this will be a terrific entry to getting an excellent job." I thought a moment. "Do you remember Norma from Olympic? She was the science teacher." Jenna remembered her well. "She teaches part of that program, and I'm sure she'll be excited to have you in her class."

I called Norma, who was happy to be my link to Jenna's progress. She was the one who, when Jenna first came to live with us, took me aside and said, "Alice, I hope you know that you are going to be the key to Jenna's success, if she actually succeeds. Others might help, but you're going to be the one who will be the center of it all." At the time I was eager to take on that responsibility. Norma had taught at-risk teens her entire career and was well aware of the low odds for kids like Jenna. After she retired from Olympic, she picked up a part-time job teaching medical terminology at the adult school.

The program was two semesters long and included an internship in which students received hands-on experience. In Jenna's class of twenty-five, all students were young women who needed a helping hand.

Jenna did remarkably well, according to Norma. She was at the top of her class and worked as an intern at the county hospital for six weeks. Her future seemed promising. Ric and I went to her graduation in May 2010. Her little boy, Jason, was there with his dad's father, who seemed to adore him. I hoped Jason's grandfather would help maintain some stability in his life. When we spoke to him, he said Brian should have been there but was home sleeping. His manner indicated he was unhappy Brian had skipped the special occasion. Jenna gave an impassioned, thankful, teary-eyed speech that reminded me of her graduation from Family Life Center. Maybe this time her newfound excitement would stick.

It didn't. The county hospital hired her but let her go within a month. Norma found out she had been frequently absent and worked half-heartedly. She didn't find another job. Then she and Brian split up. She told us he had cut up all her clothes and she needed money to replace them. She moved to a smaller apartment provided by the county. She told us she found a reliable car for $3,000, and she needed money for insurance and new tires. Her money was dwindling, and we told her it wouldn't last long unless she got a job.

One day we received an email from her that demanded all the money "that is mine." The message was in all capital letters, very unlike Jenna, and we suspected her mother had sent it. Jenna had likely reconnected with Crystal, who, in her greedy, malicious way, wanted everything she could get her hands on. We didn't respond and heard no more.

After Christmas I called the couple who had adopted Jenna's brother Brandon, who lived in Sacramento, to find out if they had heard from her. We hadn't talked to them in a long time, but I knew Jenna still had a relationship with them. Marcy, Brandon's adoptive mother, told me Jenna had spent ten days with them during the holidays. "She seemed to want to stay with us indefinitely, but I told her she needed to take care of herself and her little boy."

The last I had heard, Brandon was in a group home for violent teens; they had plenty to worry about without taking on a young mother. During the course of our conversation, I asked Marcy about Jenna's car. "What car?" she said. When I told her about Jenna's specific requests for money from us to pay for the car, tires, and insurance, I learned she had spent the money on none of them. My stomach lurched in a familiar way.

After talking it over with Ric, I called Jenna. "We recently found out you have been lying to us again," I told Jenna. "There is five thousand dollars left from the money your grandfathers left you. We'll put it in your account and let you fritter it away as you see fit."

"What are you talking about?" said Jenna.

I told her a little of my conversation with Marcy.

"You're wrong," she said. "I'm going to write you a letter and tell you everything."

"You're welcome to do that, but truly, there's no need."

We never heard from Jenna again.

As of this writing, in 2021, Jenna is thirty years old. Annie peeks at public arrest records and

Jenna's Facebook account occasionally and reports to us, even though I really don't want to know what has become of Jenna. Despite that, I learned that first, she lost Jason to foster care. There were photos of drinking and partying. Then she had another baby, who was immediately taken from her by Social Services. A Facebook post Annie saw in 2016 read, "My boyfriend, his eighteen-month-old baby, and I need a room to help us get back on our feet. Let me know if you hear of anything."

Early in 2017 Annie found an arrest record for petty theft and failure to report to work as part of probation. Recently Jenna wrote that she was moving to Las Vegas—Nevada, not the little town in New Mexico where she met some of the many people who tried their best to help her along the way.

34

Twenty-One Years Too Late

One day while visiting Sara in Martinez, Ric and I sat reading the *Contra Costa Times*. Ric nudged me and pointed to a page. "Look at this." The article was titled "Antioch Drug Dealer Sentenced to Sixteen Years in Prison for Dealing Methamphetamine." The perpetrator was Alan Wilson, thirty-nine. It couldn't be. Or could it? I Googled "Alan Wilson, Antioch Police Record," and there he was, the man who tormented Jenna when she was a little girl. His ugly, pockmocked face stared at me. Older, but undeniably him. Memories of her stories flooded back.

Alan was her brother Brandon's father, the violent man who abused her so badly. He was the one who threatened to kill Jenna if he told anyone what he did to her. Therapy had helped free her from that terror, or so she said.

Jenna stayed in touch with Brandon. He told her Alan had moved to Florida and fathered nine more children. He also told Jenna his goal was to be just like his dad.

I reflected on the abuse inflicted on Jenna through no fault of her own, beginning when she was a baby. I thought about children who lived in similar environments. Drugs, alcohol, crime, and broken homes have wreaked havoc on our society. It breaks my heart.

Alan entered Jenna's life in 1994. I saw the newspaper article in 2015. It took twenty-one years for the law to catch up with him. His sentence was for sixteen years. I wonder what will happen when he is up for parole.

Afterword

For most of my adult years, I considered myself a connector, someone who directed people to resources to help them solve problems and overcome obstacles. I was the consummate volunteer for twenty-five years, raising funds for local projects, serving on commissions and boards, and planning events. My work at Olympic High School was rewarding because the at-risk students I worked with wanted to be helped. I often told my students, "There are a lot of people who will reach out to you, but you have to grab on to their hands if you want to accept their help." I made it my mission to bring successful community members and business people into my classroom to have them interact with the students.

Then along came Jenna. Not only did she not want our help, but she seemed to want to return to the life she had before, with her despicable mother and perilous living conditions. That was what she knew. I thought she would love to live in a nice house with a caring family, make good friends, do well in school, and become a productive member of society. But that was our world, not hers. She rarely expressed her desires or fears. Her passive-aggressive behavior frustrated me to exasperation, and the way she locked up her feelings saddened me.

The most challenging aspect of Jenna was her ability to shut down and seem to have no "there, there." She almost appeared to have no soul, no inner person. How could that be?

Resilience is a word commonly associated with people who overcome adversity. Here's what the American Psychological Association says about it:

> *Resilience is the process of adapting well in the face of adversity, trauma, tragedy, threats or significant sources of stress ... It means "bouncing back" from difficult experiences.*
>
> *Research has shown that resilience is ordinary, not extraordinary. People commonly demonstrate resilience ...*
>
> *Resilience is not a trait that people either have or do not have. It involves behaviors, thoughts and actions that can be learned and developed in anyone.*[*]

---

[*]   American Psychological Association, "Building Your Resilience," 2012. https://www.apa.org/topics/resilience

That last sentence is key for me, and it's why Ric and I kept trying to help Jenna. Sadly, we learned that in extreme cases like Jenna's, only a small percentage of children who are raised in abusive environments—10 to 20 percent according to some studies—are able to overcome their adversities. In our case we found out that sometimes a person is unable to put her past behind her.

My therapist's words came back to me again and again throughout the ten years Jenna was under our care. We provided her a stable, safe home life, love, resources, and professional counseling, but she was not able to learn or develop traits that might have helped her, such as positive self-esteem, compassion, a commitment to school and other goals, trust, and the ability to connect with others. I believe she was maltreated for too many years.

Ric and I were lucky we had already raised two girls. Those impossible teenage years were old hat to us. It was easy to be firm and prepare ourselves for the worst. Sending Jenna to therapeutic boarding schools was the best thing we did for her and for us. We knew she needed professional help, and we weren't equipped to give her any more of us.

Shortly after Jenna came to live with us, Ric's work schedule changed. The refinery was bought and sold six times. A few new managers came after each sale and changed the culture of the place to the point where many of Ric's contemporaries quit. He chose to stay "until they fire me" and was relegated to duties outside the operations of the refinery—his forte—that allowed him to work forty hours a week. He no longer put his heart and soul into his work, but I loved that he was home more. We were a team with Jenna; we made decisions together and backed each other up. We gave her all we could.

We had a set term of responsibility: until Jenna turned eighteen. When the time came to let her go, I'm sure it was much easier than it would have been if she had been our own child. However, we also knew that being firm in setting limits and keeping to them is imperative for all parents. Ric's brother Mark, Jenna's father, received no favors by having his parents succumb to his continual pleas for assistance. It didn't help him, and it caused overwhelming sadness and grief for my in-laws. Once Jenna was gone from us, we were left with sad memories and a negligible sense of hope. But we did not feel we could have done any more.

Do I have regrets? None. Jenna deserved a chance to escape her past life and make a new, happy one. She was unable to. We wish Jenna the best. While I have doubts that she will ever turn herself around, there is always hope.

As for me, I have put those ten hard years behind me. After Jenna disappeared, we moved into our Boonville apartment and waited out the recession. Ric worked with Wally building custom cabinets and furniture, having a ball and improving his skills. We made friends easily in the welcoming community of Anderson Valley. I joined a women's group, took piano lessons, sang in our valley's little chorus, took writing classes in Ft. Bragg, and volunteered in the schools. Vowing to step back from major responsibilities, I joined no boards or commissions and declined to chair committees.

Building our log home was our focus for several years. Due to the recession, we reduced the size of the building, for which I was glad. While it certainly isn't a cabin in the woods, it is less imposing than it might have been and fits our needs perfectly. Ric immersed himself in the construction, doing much of the work himself. I was happy to choose floorings, colors, and furnishings. Going to the post office was like Christmas; boxes of new purchases often awaited me.

Next to my marriage to Ric and raising our two daughters, these last years have been the best of my life. Our family has expanded to include four beautiful grandchildren. We travel and spend time with friends and family, but Bonner Ridge is our refuge. I often sit on our deck with a cup of coffee or a book, gazing across Honey Creek at the ridges beyond. I am at peace, living my dream.

Acknowledgments

I have often asked myself why I chose to write this book. The story of trying to raise Jenna for ten years does not have a happy ending. Much of it is sad and depressing. The further along I got, the harder it became for me to finish. Many people have told me writing about our experiences must have been cathartic, but it actually wasn't. Ric and I were so used up by the time Jenna departed that we were left feeling no emotions toward her.

My writing teacher, Norma Watkins, and my classmates at Mendocino College in Ft. Bragg, California, encouraged me to share my experiences, not only so others could learn about how difficult raising an abused child can be, but to describe my own growth. They were immensely supportive. I couldn't have had a more stimulating and fun group to work with. Lisa Locascio, writer extraordinaire, gave me insightful developmental editing along the way. Later, members of my writing group, Catherine Marshall, Orah Young, Robyn Koski, and Karin Uphoff, reinvigorated me to finish the book after I set it down for some three years. My brother Jerry and friends Tom Boggess, Brenda Roberts, Carol Fidler, Patti Hanson, Barrie Eddy, and Lauri Carrick—who spent considerable time reading, making suggestions, and editing—gave me courage to publish the work. Thank you all. I also have great regard and am grateful for the expertise of Sheridan McCarthy and Stanton Nelson of Meadowlark Publishing Services. They were patient, helpful, and experienced within the daunting world of self-publishing. They taught me more than I ever wanted to know about the Chicago style of writing. Most of all, I am thankful for Ric, Sara, and Annie, who held me together when I felt I was falling apart during those ten years, and who have supported me throughout the writing of this story.

About the Author

Releasing Jenna is the author's first book. After joining a creative writing class, she felt compelled to write about her family's experiences raising Jenna, her niece. The teacher and students in the class encouraged Alice to compile all the stories about Jenna and publish this book.

Alice is a native Californian who grew up in a stable, loving family. Although she worked with at-risk teens, she had no concept of what it would be like to welcome into her home a young girl who had been abused in multiple ways since birth.

After their retirement, Alice and her husband built a quiet mountain retreat in the woods of northern California. She lives there in the small community of Boonville in Mendocino County.